I0816935

Praise for Danish Kurani's *The Spaces That Make Us*

"Danish Kurani is one of the industry's most exciting, innovative figures. His ideas changed how I see the world and interact with my surroundings. This book is an eye-opener for anyone who loves design—or simply wants a happier life."

—Paul Makovsky, editor in chief of *ARCHITECT* magazine

"In his new book, Kurani introduces a world-changing design philosophy that will inspire readers to craft their ideal world. In doing so, he reveals how as we shape our spaces, our spaces then shape us."

—Debbie Millman, host of *Design Matters*

"A heartfelt, deeply researched book. *The Spaces That Make Us* shows that how we choose to design our surroundings shapes who we become. We can all become the architects of our own lives should we choose to dream courageously."

—Sheena Iyengar, Columbia Business School professor and bestselling author of *The Art of Choosing*

"*The Spaces That Make Us* is a beautiful and powerful reminder that our health, happiness, and even identities are the product of hidden forces all around us. Danish Kurani shows how to design spaces that transform us into the people we want to be. You'll never see the physical world the same way again."

—Jonah Berger, *New York Times* bestselling author of *Contagious* and *The Catalyst*

"An engaging read and a powerful argument that the best design grows out of generous attention to human need and deep regard for place."

—Sam Lubell, *New York Times* contributor

"*The Spaces That Make Us* is an exceptional work that reimagines how smart, ethical, thoughtful design can radically change our lives. I want to live in that world."

—Rachel Sonis, *TIME* magazine

"Kurani has no illusions about the forces conspiring to make our world uglier, yet this is an undeniably hopeful book. With deep care and precision, he argues for a revolutionary reimagining of the places we call home. It's a delight to join him on the journey."

—James Rodriguez, *Business Insider*

"An uncommonly accessible book about architecture that pulls the focus away from buildings to show how design shapes people's experience of the world. It's a passionate call to use that power for good."

—Nate Berg, *Fast Company*

THE SPACES THAT MAKE US

Why Design Is Broken and How We Can Create a Happier, Healthier World

DANISH KURANI

WITH CHRIS WELLER

The Spaces That Make Us

Published by Harper Celebrate, an imprint of HarperCollins Focus LLC, 501 Nelson Place, Nashville, TN 37214, USA.

All illustrations sketched by Danish Kurani and digitally recreated by Nikita Mahajan.

Cover design by Micah Kandros
Interior design by Emily Ghattas and Kristy Edwards
Headshot photography by Chase Anderson

HarperCollins Publishers, Macken House, 39/40 Mayor Street Upper, Dublin 1, D01 C9W8, Ireland (https://www.harpercollins.com)

ISBN 978-1-4002-4912-1 (HC)
ISBN 978-1-4002-4915-2 (audio)
ISBN 978-1-4002-4919-0 (ebook)

Printed in Malaysia

25 26 27 28 29 OFF 5 4 3 2 1

The ultimate hidden truth of the world
is that it is something that we make,
and could just as easily make differently.

—David Graeber, anthropologist

CONTENTS

Part 1 - The Problem

Part 2 - The Solution

Part 3 - Baaham in Action

Part 4 - Let's Get to Work

PART 1

THE PROBLEM

The first part of this book demonstrates how far our species has strayed from its ancient architectural instincts in the ways we currently design. By understanding the forces and mindsets behind modern design, you can move forward more intentionally to devise solutions that make life better, not worse, for yourself and others.

1

A WORLD SICK WITH BAD DESIGN

We're living in a suboptimal world that we designed. It's up to us to redesign it.

HIGH SPEED, HIGH STAKES

At around 9 p.m. on December 24, 1998, my young body was flung from the back seat of a Toyota Corolla, over the passenger seat, and into the car windshield.

I was thirteen years old.

The bad news was that my mom suffered a broken leg, my sister and I sustained bruises on our faces and arms, and the car was totaled. The good news is that I'm still alive to tell you how it all happened—and how a bad design nearly got us killed.

A year before the crash, my parents had gotten divorced. During that time, I moved with my mom and younger sister eleven miles south of our hometown. But the mosque we had belonged to for most of my life was back in our old town. Since we didn't want to leave our entire community behind, a couple times each week, the three of us would pile into our navy blue Corolla and make the twenty-minute trip north along a local highway. Then, after evening prayer services were over, we would make the same trip home.

Thursday, December 24, went a little differently.

It was drizzling that night and pitch-black except for the hazy headlights of a few other drivers and an occasional light from a gas station. When we were about fifteen minutes from home, we approached an intersection we'd passed dozens of times before. The intersection allowed cars from perpendicular side streets to merge onto or cross the highway. My sister, six years old at the time, was sitting in the back seat behind my mom in the driver's seat. I was next to my sister, behind the empty passenger seat. One moment we were driving along, talking to each other, and the next moment my ninety-seven-pound body was flying headfirst through the air and crashing into the windshield. I was not wearing my seat belt. The next thing I remember was opening my eyes and finding myself balled up in the front of the car, feeling a mixture of shock and bewilderment.

What just happened?

I looked at my mom. She was slumped over the steering wheel, pinned between the seat and the dashboard. Somehow she was alert enough to calmly instruct me to get out of the car and call 911. I can't remember if I opened the dented door or shimmied through an open window; all I know is I managed to crawl out like my mom had instructed. I stumbled, then gained my composure as a crowd of people began encircling our car. Raindrops pelted my face. I yelled out, "Someone call 911!" A nice man with a cell phone offered to dial for me.

While he made the call, I was finally able to take in the full scene: two cars crumpled like discarded soda cans, ours pushed halfway into the grassy median. Several yards away, I observed the black SUV that hit us. Its front end was hanging off like a broken jaw. I figured the driver must not have seen our car. Or perhaps they thought they could cross to the other side fast enough so they pulled out right as we were speeding down the highway at fifty-five miles per hour.

Force = mass x acceleration took care of the rest.

When the paramedics and fire department arrived, they lifted me and my sister into the back of a fire truck, where we sat and watched through the windows as they pulled my mom from the wreckage. I held my sister close, both of us staring at the blurry flashing lights outside. The worst thoughts came to mind: *Is Mom going to be okay? What happens to us if she's not?* At one point, the truck began moving. We were terrified, but at least we were leaving the chaos behind.

The next six months were some of the hardest I had ever faced up to that point. The night of the crash, in the hospital, we learned that my mom had snapped both the tibia and fibula in her left leg clean through. Now, with a bulky cast up to her knee, she was immobile. It was up to my sister and me to take care of ourselves. It helped that my mother's friends from our mosque brought us meals, cared for my mom, and took over some basic household chores. But without my mom to drive me places, I missed a lot of social events. As a thirteen-year-old, I wouldn't process what this meant until many years later. Looking back, I can see that this event marked the end of my childhood. I became the man of the house.

When my mom's cast came off, I thought we were closing that awful chapter, that all the memories of the accident would fade. But the trauma of that night plagued my body long after the event. For me, that trauma surfaced through sound. Every time we went for a drive and I heard a car speed past, my body would shiver. I would tense up and hold my breath, as if bracing for impact, until the car was long gone. It would be another fifteen years, into my late twenties, before some of that trauma was released and the shivering stopped.

Accidents happen. But what I want to know is, why do we call car crashes *accidents*?

I think it's because we know humans are error prone. We assume that drivers sometimes get distracted or take unnecessary risks or lose control. For a long time, that's the explanation our family accepted about that crash on the way home from the mosque. We were proceeding safely along the road when another driver made what they thought was a safe decision that turned out to be wrong.

As I've processed those events—and as I've learned more about the world we live in—I don't think that's the right story. My mom and the other driver weren't the only two factors that determined whether cars were at risk of crashing that night. I believe something even greater was at fault: the design of the road. Instead of a traffic light, the intersection had a stop sign. This required drivers from side streets to judge for themselves when it was safe to merge onto or cross the four lanes of highway. All of this and on a pitch-black road without a single streetlight.

We call them *accidents*, but how many crashes could we prevent if our roads were better designed? In my opinion, the traffic engineers and civil engineers who designed that intersection deserve as much blame as the driver who hit us. If they had considered the possibility that, at some point, one driver might misjudge how fast an oncoming car is traveling, they might have realized that a traffic light would be better than a stop sign.

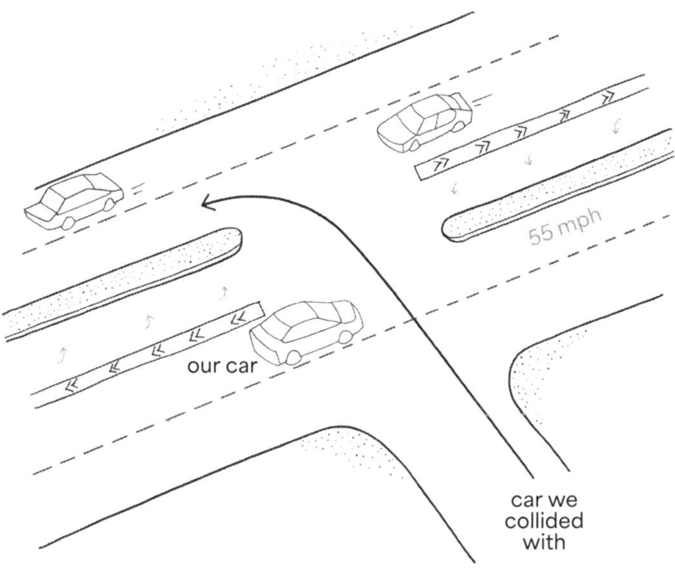

If they had, we probably would have arrived home safely that night. December 24, 1998, would have been lost to history, like any other Thursday. Instead, it has become a chilling reminder of when it all could have ended.

+ + +

When it comes to how our world is designed, the poor design of a dangerous intersection isn't an anomaly; it's the norm. And while bad design can ruin your life in dramatic fashion, snapping your leg in half in a car crash, more often it's the gradual bleed you don't really notice, like disrupted sleep because your bedroom lets in the sounds of humming household appliances or revving traffic outside. There's mounting evidence to suggest that these bad designs are damaging our health, relationships, thinking, and quality of life.

In schools, the poor acoustics of many classrooms make it difficult for students to hear what their instructor is teaching. Because of these poor acoustics, students may miss up to 25 percent of what's being taught, causing them to fall behind.[1] Excess classroom noise also makes teaching more stressful for instructors and can cause temporary or permanent vocal fatigue, strain, or damage.[2] Other studies show how poor lighting can disrupt a student's hormones, make them more fidgety, and hurt their academic performance.[3]

In a hospital, if your room looks toward a blank wall, you're more likely to need stronger doses of painkillers and have a longer recovery time than someone whose room faces nature. You're also more likely to experience anxiety and stress throughout the day compared to the nature-facing patients, who are more likely to feel a sense of calm and peace.[4]

How we travel between places also affects our emotions, physical health, and perception of others. While riding public transportation, when there's a delay, we can commiserate and feel like "we're all in this together." But when driving in cars, we're up against others who take the space we need. Fellow citizens become antagonists rather than allies.

Concerning physical health, by living in neighborhoods that are not walkable, we face greater risks of diabetes, obesity, and cancer.[5] And when we must drive in rush-hour traffic, on the heaviest traffic days, our likelihood of committing domestic violence goes up by 9 percent.[6]

When our spaces aren't well designed, they limit our potential, destroy our health, and bring out our worst qualities. Without realizing it, we've created a world that is ugly, aggressive, and detrimental to our lives. Lucky for us, this suboptimal world is one that *we* designed, which means we can *re*design it.

THE MYTH ABOUT WHAT MATTERS

The challenging part is that it's difficult to turn things around when we don't fully understand the purpose of architecture. In America, we're misled by celebrity "design experts," who give us the impression that design is all about looks. We're taught to treat design as if it's a piece of clothing—a way to express ourselves and nothing more. At the very least, shouldn't we create something comfortable to wear? But with such an insistence on looking good, we've created the opposite. We're living in an uncomfortable gala dress, our toes blistered from squeezing into high heels. This is no way to live.

Without realizing it, we've created a world that is ugly, aggressive, and detrimental to our lives.

We should care how our architecture fits because we're surrounded by it at nearly every moment. Our lives are contained inside it. Still, when I say *architecture* in conversation, people usually picture sleek high-rises or majestic museums and religious centers. But architecture is more than fancy, celebrated buildings. Every inch of the built environment—every doorknob you turn, every window you look through, every building you love or hate or notice or don't notice, every warehouse, parking structure, and bridge, and every space in between—all of these are architecture.

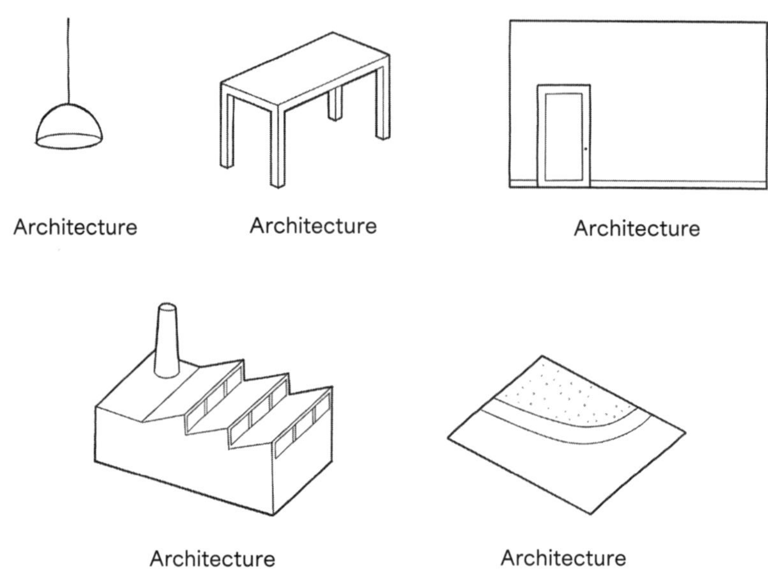

Though we engage with architecture every day, we rarely stop to consider: *How does my environment affect my health and productivity? My happiness and relationships? My emotions and behavior?* Because built spaces have always been part of our lives, we've forgotten that they're influencing us every minute. So when we fail in some way, it's not necessarily our fault. It could very well be that our environment didn't set us up for success. Writer and architect Christopher Alexander explained it well: "There is a myth, sometimes widespread, that . . . a man is entirely responsible for his own problems . . . that the individual is self-sufficient, and not dependent in any essential way on his surroundings. The fact is, a person is so far formed by his surroundings, that his state of harmony depends entirely on his harmony with his surroundings."[7] Perhaps we forget that this is a major reason we build in the first place: to create a state of tranquillity for ourselves.

We need architecture that creates harmony in our chaotic world. As psychologist Mihaly Csikszentmihalyi says: "The universe was not designed with the comfort of human beings in mind . . . most of it is hostilely empty and cold. . . . Even planet Earth, which can be so idyllic and picturesque, is not to be taken for granted. To survive on it men and women have had to struggle for millions of years against ice, fire, floods, wild animals, and invisible microorganisms that appear out of nowhere to snuff us out."[8]

So we must build to solve our problems. The word *design* itself comes from the fourteenth-century Latin *designare*, meaning "to contrive" or "plot." This approach to design is what makes a difference in people's lives. We should be asking how we can transform our built world so that it's helping us, not hurting us. The spaces we design today guide how we live tomorrow. The design of our homes, offices, schools, grocery stores, and hospitals, along with the many other places we depend on every day, influences us immeasurably.

Architecture is more than walls and roofs; it's how we shape our lives. And yet TV shows and social media posts are telling us to focus on style and appearance. They're blinding us with superficial cosmetic touches. We may sense that something feels wrong but don't know quite how to address it. How can we fix our environments so they're life-affirming and supportive?

Each of us can redesign this world for ourselves. All we need is a blueprint for how to design *well.* This book offers that blueprint.

A NEW PHILOSOPHY

This book describes an entirely different attitude to architecture. It's intended to provide a humanistic alternative to our present ideas about architecture, building, and planning—an alternative that, I hope, will gradually replace our current thinking and practices.

This book attempts to show what happens to people's quality of life when we design for certain outcomes—when we stop thinking of design as a way to make the world *look* a certain way and start thinking about it as a tool to make the world *work* a certain way. Better yet, it attempts to show how design can help us all create the life we most want to live. You'll see how our homes affect our relationships with our families and neighbors, how grocery stores manipulate us into buying overpriced junk food, and how schools create distracting and unproductive learning environments—and then you'll be empowered to make more informed choices to create better outcomes for you and the people you care about.

What this book is *not* is the typical set of prescriptions for how you should design your home. Instead, it's a tool to help you think about how to design the best space for *you*, in whichever style you prefer. It's not about how to build cheaper or faster using the latest tools and technology. It's about considering *why* we build in the first place—because *what* and *how* we build only matter if we're clear on *why* we're building.

Ever since I can remember, I've been obsessed with our built environment. I think about physical space every hour I'm awake, whether it's the height of a coffee table, the accessibility of a park, or the design of a street; whether it's getting a better night's sleep, improving my relationship with my partner, or focusing more at work. This obsession has endowed me with something of a superpower. Similar to the way Sherlock Holmes can take one glance at a murder scene, assemble clues like puzzle pieces, and imagine how the crime unfolded, I can piece together the impacts of a space. Others may see an ordinary desk or window, but I see how those objects are influencing the people in that space.

This book is about inviting you inside my mind to see those forces at work—because once you understand them, you'll notice your own surroundings and will want to begin designing spaces to optimize your life. This book is intended to be accessible for everyone—everyday people, people with influence, designers, and nondesigners alike—because each of us has a stake in how our world is designed.

Early in the book, I'm going to take you on a journey, one that begins with our primitive ancestors building shelters to meet their basic needs. From there, we'll see how industrialization and mass production, particularly as they've taken shape in the United States, have degraded our relationship with design. Finally, we'll make our way to the present to see how celebrities and corporations use social media to promote products and design trends that don't actually improve your life.

Once you understand the problems we're facing, we'll explore the design philosophy I've developed and used over the past twenty-five years, honing it through my research and practice, including running my own design studio. That philosophy is *Baaham*. An esoteric word in my native language Urdu, *baaham* essentially means "two things working together, in tandem, and influencing each other," and, to me, reflects the reciprocity between us and our physical environments. First, we make our spaces; then our spaces make us.

This book marks the first time I'm sharing the practice of Baaham design with the general public. I want to offer access to the same tools I rely on as a designer, such as focusing on solving problems before considering aesthetics and zooming out to consider the relationships between people and objects. Want to boost your confidence by changing the lighting in your bathroom? Want to become more creative by moving your desk? Want to feel cool in the summer without blasting the air conditioning? I can show you how design accomplishes all of that—and more.

In the middle chapters, I'll explain each Baaham principle and offer helpful mindsets you can adopt along with activities you can practice. Think of this section as your personal reference guide that you can revisit anytime a new project comes along.

Toward the end of the book, we'll begin to imagine what a world built with Baaham could look like. We'll walk through the process of designing a Baaham home, workplace, school, and hospital, and finally, an entire Baaham community. Given the current state of design, these visions of a Baaham world may feel like a fantasy at first—a naïve utopian dream. You alone may not have the power to fix every problem of design or transform the planet, but I invite you to notice the possibilities that surround you as you begin to understand the power of Baaham.

In the final chapter, we'll step back into our daily lives and consider how we can begin applying the wisdom of Baaham wherever we find ourselves. We've all experienced the effects of bad architecture: when a school fails to lift students, when an office turns a passion into a chore, when a neighborhood makes it impossible to be healthy. It's up to us to recognize the roles we play, the changes we're capable of making to our surroundings, and how we can do better in those roles. Whether you're a designer, real estate developer, businessperson, or government official; whether you're a parent, community leader, or concerned citizen; we all bear a responsibility to start building a better world for ourselves.

It may take a while before you reach a Sherlock Holmes–level of intuition, where you can walk into a room and immediately see its potential, but I'm confident that over time, with the right mindset, you'll find that design becomes a gut instinct or even a magical superpower. Whatever happens, I know one thing is true: By the time you finish reading this book, you will never see your physical world the same again. You will have true architectural awareness.

That's my goal: to empower you with awareness to design better spaces. Even if you think you don't have the ability to make a difference because you feel trapped inside a system that's too large to dismantle or with too small a budget, I assure you: Together we can. Come with me, and I'll show you how we each have a part to play in redesigning our world. All I ask is that you keep an open mind along the journey. Whether we intend it or not, design changes people's lives. Shouldn't we use it to make lives better?

If we don't—if we continue building suboptimal spaces for living, working, learning, healing, and socializing—we'll not only be products of our environments; we'll also be victims of them.

Residents in my hometown were lucky to finally have a traffic light installed at that dangerous intersection, but it took far too long and, frankly, came too late. The driver of a heavy SUV was forced to make a split-second decision, at night, in the rain, about whether our car was far enough away to safely cross the highway. Because of that decision, our lives were never the same. And I learned an unforgettable lesson: Design matters.

Whether we intend it or not, design changes people's lives. Shouldn't we use it to make lives better?

I'm on a journey to redesign our built world to prevent life-shattering events like these from happening and to replace them, instead, with the kind of world we dream of. But I can't take this journey alone.

Will you join me?

2

TO BE HUMAN IS TO ARCHITECT

We used to build architecture to take care of our needs. Lately we've forgotten its purpose.

ARCHITECTURE MAKES US HUMAN

Imagine it's 2,000,000 BCE. Earth is blanketed in lush forests and diverse ecosystems. Prehistoric birds chirp; insects buzz; predators howl. Near the base of a tree, a group of primates sleeps soundly in a nest. The nest is fashioned from a woven pile of sticks and brush. It may seem like an ordinary ground nest, but it's a form of architecture that will go on to play a critical role in our evolution as human beings.

Before primates slept on the ground, they slept in trees. But tree-dwelling monkeys don't sleep like humans do, because when a monkey sleeps in a tree, its brain never fully turns off. A small part of the animal's brain stays alert to help it maintain a sense of balance.[1] If the monkey did fall into a deep sleep, a gust of wind could send the snoozing monkey tumbling to the forest floor below. It wasn't until a band of particularly adventurous primates came down from the trees and built their nests and communities on the earth floor that these primates got their first dose of deep sleep. Once they did, everything changed.

With the comfort of a built shelter and the protection of fellow group members, these ground-dwelling primates were rewarded with the benefits of deep sleep. During deep sleep, the brain can fully recharge. It removes cognitive waste and enables the formation of more sophisticated brain structures. As time went on, these advantages unlocked higher-order thinking and problem-solving among the primates, ultimately allowing for the evolution into modern-day humans.

Think about that for a moment.

All thanks to ground-based nests—a simple form of architecture—we began to sleep deeply, and our brains evolved from simple pattern-recognition machines into the marvels that eventually figured out organ transplants, satellite communication, and cloning. Architecture was a key factor in our evolutionary development, and it made way for these innovations to come. Our evolution from tree-dwelling primates to ground-dwelling human primates wouldn't be the last time our ancestors used architecture to support their survival.

Fast-forward to 15,000 BCE. The planet is home to many different species of humans, all coexisting with one another. One group, the Homo sapiens, has left behind the hunter-gatherer lifestyle and begun to seek out more permanent settlements. They've started building fences to contain the crops and livestock they use to barter with their neighbors. Again, we see architecture used as a tool to solve problems. Our ancestors learned, often the hard way, that hunting and foraging for food came with risks. Sometimes they'd find nothing but inedible or poisonous plants, and sometimes an ambush would quickly turn them from predator to prey. They were able to reduce their risks through architecture—creating fences that contained their plants and animals—thereby giving them more control over what they could grow, eat, and trade. Architecture gave them control over how they lived.

Throughout history, architecture has supported our evolution as a species. Without it, we might all still be clinging to tree branches for dear life, half asleep.

CARRYING ON THE ARCHITECTURAL INSTINCT

Even as our species figured out how to construct growing villages and thriving metropolises, from ancient Rome through the Renaissance, we kept sight of those early instincts to build for our needs. As recently as the 1850s, we saw our architectural instincts at work in the decades-long reconstruction of Paris.

Today, the French capital city is known for its fashion and beauty.

Paris, 1840s

But in the middle of the 1800s, Paris was a city of squalor and disease. Because of an economic boom, between 1815 and 1853, the city's population had doubled. Twice, in 1832 and 1848, Paris experienced a deadly cholera epidemic. With overpopulation and antiquated sewage infrastructure, Parisians were living in dark, cramped alleys and were dumping their waste in the Seine River, which led to the spread of infectious diseases. Many of these health issues arose because of the city's layout, first developed during the Middle Ages. By the 1800s, this inadequate layout was already several hundred years out of date. Basic resources like water and natural gas couldn't reach the surging populace. Congested roads created

Paris, 1860s

terrible pollution that choked residents with no space to breathe. Life in Paris was a public health nightmare.

In 1853, French officials decided enough was enough. They asked Georges-Eugène Haussmann, a twenty-year veteran in public administration, to lead a total transformation of the city's design. Haussmann, together with French president Napoleon III (not to be confused with his uncle Napoleon Bonaparte) and thousands of French workers, undertook several key projects. They tore down congested and crumbling buildings to make room for pedestrian sidewalks, added twenty-four public squares and forty-nine hundred acres of parks, planted six hundred thousand trees, installed a state-of-the-art underground sewage system, and quadrupled the width of most roads, establishing airy boulevards and effectively giving the city lungs to breathe. A parliamentary report from 1859 stated the project "brought air, light, and healthiness" to the city.

The new Paris was open, accessible, clean, and becoming disease-free.

The lesson from the redesign of Paris in the 1850s, much like the lessons from our ancient ancestors, is that architecture is a tool that can solve our problems. When we encounter challenges, or opportunities for a better life, we can use design and architecture to promote new and better ways of living.

But think about how remarkable a project like the redesign of Paris seems now. How often do cities today identify their major social or public health problems and consider design as a tool to solve them? Especially in America, that mindset seems to have gone missing.

THE PROLIFERATION OF "PREMADE"

As recently as the 1860s, if you lived outside a major metropolis and your family needed a place to live, you and your community would band together to build that home yourselves. You'd think about how the home could best serve your family's needs. If you were a farmer, you built all the structures that made sense for a farmer's way of life. If you were a fisherman or merchant, you built a home suited to *your* lifestyle. And you used materials available to you locally. It was all very practical. By the 1870s, however, America was quickly adopting a new way of building—and not just architecture but everyday items. We stopped making things individually by hand and started making them en masse with machines.

The Industrial Revolution forever changed how we create everyday products. We began mass-producing most goods, including clothing, furniture, automobiles, and food. Borrowing the Latin word *factor*, meaning "doer" or "maker," we invented a building whose capabilities in speed and quantity far surpassed the outputs of mere humans: the almighty factory. Mechanical efficiency and higher production volumes lowered prices, giving everyday citizens access to products they previously couldn't afford.

Architecture, too, became mass-produced.

In 1908, under its "Modern Homes" program, the department store Sears began selling kits of precut lumber, loose parts, and assembly manuals in its mail-order catalogs. Americans no longer had to design. Instead, they could pick out a predesigned home simply by tearing out a flier and sending a check to their local department store. In thirty years, Sears Modern Homes sold approximately seventy-five thousand predesigned homes.

While the Sears home kits—and mass production—made it easier for people to erect a home, which was a benefit, it came with a trade-off: We began outsourcing the *thinking* about how our spaces should be designed. This reflected a key shift in our attitude toward design. People were no longer living in homes that were as suited to their needs as the ones they used to design for themselves. Instead, they began living in structures that corporations designed for a hypothetical family. Gradual as the shift was, outsourcing our thinking was a mistake and one that has continued to haunt us. We have stopped using our architectural instinct and have given corporations the right to design how we live and what our day-to-day lives will feel like.

As novel as the Sears Modern Homes program was, its true impact was laying a foundation for a much larger change after World War II. Real estate development, as its own industry, took off in the postwar boom of the 1950s. With veterans returning from overseas and families looking to settle down, the mid-1900s saw the rise of not only mass-produced homes but mass-produced neighborhoods.

We have stopped using our architectural instinct and have given corporations the right to design how we live and what our day-to-day lives will feel like.

The most famous examples are the ones started by William J. Levitt, a property developer who opened the first "Levittown" in Long Island, New York. The development included thousands of mass-produced homes that Levitt had assembled according to a process modeled off factory assembly lines. Each house was identical to the next, each unit fully furnished with all-new appliances. They were marketed as the perfect home for soldiers returning from overseas.

Within the first few hours of offering these initial Long Island homes, Levitt had sold more than fourteen hundred units. Between 1947 and 1964, he'd go on to sell tens of thousands more and open new "Levittowns" in Pennsylvania, New Jersey, Maryland, and even Puerto Rico. These developments soon became the standard for suburban neighborhoods across the U.S.

By the sixties, seventies, and eighties, it had become normal for American families to go through the same process for finding a new home. If you weren't building a custom home, you were probably given a tour of a neighborhood that a speculative developer had already built and asked which home you liked best. Whichever home caught your eye the most was the one you likely chose.

Like Levitt's homes, these designs were created without the homeowner's input. But unlike Levitt's homes, whose purpose was giving unhoused soldiers a place to live, the houses in the decades following the postwar boom weren't built to solve a problem. They were built to minimize choice and maximize profits. Developers benefited from a society that had abandoned its architectural instincts and become not just willing but grateful for the chance to buy a cookie-cutter home.

The shift marked a stunning transformation from two million years ago, and it was only picking up steam. Postwar America saw a transition from partially outsourcing the thinking of what's best for us to fully outsourcing it. We were being given architecture built with minimal thought paid to our needs, yet it was packaged and sold as the American Dream.

COLLECTING (AND COPYING) DESIGNS

As the postwar boom progressed, so did the erosion of our architectural instincts. This erosion took place everywhere we traveled—and travel we did. In 1950, global airline passengers numbered around 19 million. But by 1969, that figure had soared to approximately 289 million passengers. The era of mass air travel—and mass design copying—had arrived.

With access to airliners that could now make long-distance flights, wealthier citizens could jet-set to the beachfront bungalows of Hawaii or the wintery mountain lodges of Switzerland. They could tour the charming traditional flats of London or the tranquil tea houses of Japan. In each place, they saw exotic buildings, furniture, and styles of construction they had never seen before and developed an affinity for those discoveries. The memory of these treasured items soon became the inspiration for their upcoming design projects and home renovations.

The problem was that people weren't copying solutions; they were copying styles. They weren't paying attention to how a design worked in a particular place; they were paying attention to how it looked. People brought home ideas from afar that didn't make sense for their lives, like when people from colder cities in the American Northeast took trips to Southern cities like Charleston and Atlanta and fell in love with homes featuring double-height spaces. When it came time to move into a new home, those dreams of tall spaces came rushing back, and homebuyers would ask their builders for those same tall spaces, forgetting that heat rises. During the harsh Northeast winter, the heat inside their homes would move up toward the high ceiling, leaving them chilly down below. The same feature that keeps Southern homes cool in the summer makes life unbearable in a colder climate in the winter.

Copying as we traveled continued for another fifty years, until the next shift in how the world discovered design: the advent of the internet. It's hard to overstate the impact the internet has had on the way we consume and build architecture. In the mid-1800s, mass media gave people only the occasional glimpse into what life was like elsewhere—in newspapers, magazines, books, and posters. Traveling by ship or steam engine was expensive and time-consuming, and it wasn't until the 1950s and '60s that people began widely copying the styles they had seen up close with their own two eyes.

The internet changed all that, accelerating our copying. Now we have the power to copy styles without even visiting a place. Looking at a flat image on the screen, we can "copy" the design of a 3-D place and never stop to consider why it was designed that way and whether it makes sense for our needs, climate, and culture. Since the early 2000s, we have been able to copy based purely on a photograph and one-click-buy the elements of that design right away, no architectural instincts required.

AN INSTINCT ON THE VERGE OF EXTINCTION

So to recap the last two million years, while we started off as natural architects, constantly thinking about our needs and how to build for them, we've lost our way. You can still find examples of architects, designers, urbanists, and sociologists fiercely devoted to thinking about how we interact with our spaces. But as a rule, we've stopped thinking about our own architecture so that others can do it for us—and they don't always have our best interests in mind.

For most of history, architecture emerged out of need. Our ancestors used architecture to solve problems. It was all very personal. Each person had a problem and created structures to solve that problem. But slowly, we've stopped thinking critically about why we're building. It's astonishing that we've discovered atoms, engineered tiny robots that can enter our bodies to perform surgery, and propelled into outer space—yet we still have offices where we struggle to focus and playgrounds where our kids can't safely play. Our technical skills are improving, but our design skills are regressing.

Deep within us, we all have an instinct to design and solve problems, but it will wither away if we don't catch ourselves and resist the modern, systematic pull toward bad design.

3

THE MACHINE OF BAD DESIGN

Design media, retail, and real estate are all selling us junk.

A MISEDUCATION IN DESIGN

On a Saturday morning not too long ago, I called my younger sister to catch up about her week.

My sister lives in a typical American suburb in the Southeast. Eight months earlier, she'd bought a new home. And on this particular Saturday, she had a problem. Despite falling in love with her house in early January, it was now August, which meant temperatures were pushing into the mid-nineties, and her house was baking. Even with the air conditioning at full blast, my sister complained that her office upstairs felt suffocating.

"I'll even turn on the air conditioning upstairs when I'm hanging out downstairs," she told me. "That way it's cool by the time I need to go up there."

I'd seen this movie before. When my family moved from Pakistan to Atlanta, Georgia, we came to learn that air conditioning in the summer was as necessary as clean drinking water. To this day, I know people all over the South, from muggy Miami to dry Dallas, who continually run their AC regardless of which room they're in. Even though it spikes their electric bill and is environmentally detrimental, that's just the cost of coping with a bad design.

As an architect, I've learned that air conditioning isn't our only option for staying cool. We can use smarter design to cool our homes, no electricity required, just as people in hot climates like Africa and the Middle East have for thousands of years.[1] This was news to my sister.

"Wait, how does that work?" she asked.

I explained how design features like trees and roof overhangs shade the home; well-placed windows catch ventilating crosswind breezes; better insulation keeps the interiors more temperate; and awnings over windows keep the sun off the glass, where heat enters the home.

There was a long pause on the other end of the line.

"Are you still there?" I asked.

"This is honestly blowing my mind," my sister said. "I just thought that because it's a brand-new house, it'd be energy efficient."

My sister is no dummy. She has her PhD in biomedical sciences from the nation's leading health institution. She's considered exceptional in her field. But I wasn't surprised by her reaction. Most people never learn that heating and air conditioning are solutions to problems *we've created for ourselves.*

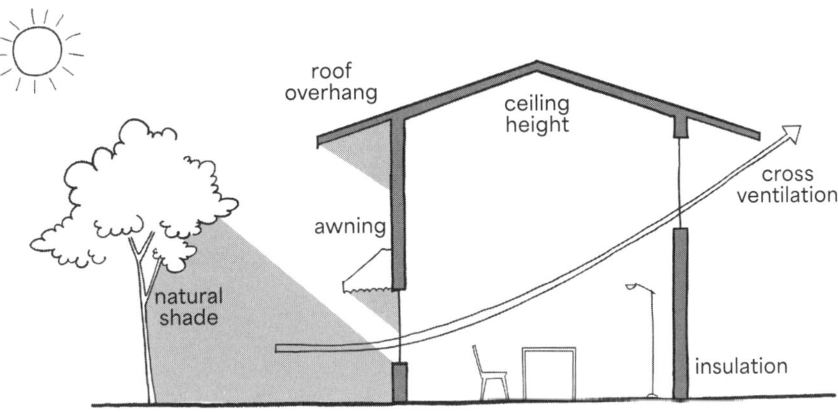

If your primary mode of learning about design is through home renovation shows, tips in decor magazines, and posts on social media, you may never learn that a home's design can keep it a comfortable temperature all year long. You get only a partial education.

I see these effects whenever I visit my sister's house. Many of her home's features and decorations were inspired by trendy design content. Her dining room, for example, was built with a statement lighting fixture—an ornate chandelier—because a TV show told everyone it would elevate the look of the room. Except the chandelier was installed without carefully considering the room's layout, and it protrudes into the walking space and makes you feel like you'll hit your head—a fault of the home developer who installed it without much thought. In her kitchen, there's a marble-top island because so many shows say it's the stylish thing to do. But the island top has no overhang, so your knees knock into the side of the island when you're sitting on a stool.

Each of these pains was preventable if the social media feeds, TV shows, and other forms of design content my sister had consumed prior to the buying process had taught her better. But they didn't, because the shows she watches, the articles she reads, and the social media stars she follows generally don't educate her, or anyone else, on how to become smarter about design or how to advocate for what really matters.

The developer who built her house didn't see it as their job to educate her either. And when she goes into her favorite furniture stores—stores that millions of people turn to for home furnishings—none of their employees is going to tell her she's buying the wrong furniture.

These three groups—design media, real estate, and retail—are the forces today that lead us to create poor physical environments. Together, they make up the machine of bad design. As we'll see, power brokers in each of these three groups aren't driven by improving people's lives. They're driven by profits. Their goal is not to solve your problems. Their goal is to make money, and they do it by selling us what we're told we need, not what we *actually* need.

While no single person is solely responsible for the effects of the machine of bad design, if you're in these industries, I invite you to think about how you help or hurt consumers. Even if you're stuck in the middle of a system that feels unchangeable, ask yourself: *What steps can I take to make life better for my customers, clients, and followers?* Even if you don't believe you're part of the problem, how can you be part of the solution?

A concerted effort is what we need because the machine of bad design ensures that we, the consumers, crave whatever the people at the top create. In most cases, they know that what they're selling is junk that creates unnecessary headaches and ultimately makes life more difficult. But as long as we keep buying it, they'll keep producing it.

We can escape this vicious cycle only if we educate ourselves and start demanding more from the people who keep the machine running. We must demand *better.*

NOT A SOLUTION IN SIGHT

Here's a statistic that may surprise you: As of this writing, home design shows are among the most popular cable TV programs in America, behind only news and sports. Just a few years ago, they became the second-most-watched programs on cable, trailing only the news.

The optimist in me sees this popularity as an opportunity to educate a captive audience on how design can improve people's lives. But the realist in me knows the truth: Thoughtful professional designers and architects are almost nowhere to be found on these programs. Pick a design show at random, and chances are the host, or hosts, fit into one of two categories: Either they are a decorator, or they are a home flipper. Both types can lead to bad outcomes.

Decorators are concerned mainly with the visual outcome of the space. They may take a boring or cluttered home and spruce it up—swapping the old furniture for something new and modern, replacing the wood cabinets with open shelving—but their modifications are generally cosmetic. Their job is to create the most emotional "reveal" moment possible, when the homeowners take off their blindfolds and see a transformed living room. The drama of such a makeover attracts millions of repeat viewers and boosts ratings.

The home flippers, meanwhile, care most about resale value. When they take an abandoned home and start ripping down walls in a gut renovation, their goal is turning the property into something that will earn them a return on their investment. Their job as entertainers is to keep the viewer in suspense. *Will the project come under budget? Will the finished product sell? How much can the home's market value increase?*

From my perspective, in both cases, whether the new home meets anybody's needs is often largely irrelevant. Decorators operate on a superficial level. House flippers operate on a speculative, financial level. So who's thinking about the experiential level? Who's thinking about whether the transformed home will ultimately make the homeowner happier, healthier, and more fulfilled beyond the big reveal? While they might be using design to make a space more stunning, they don't seem to regard design as a tool to make life better.

What concerns me even more is that the celebrity hosts you see on TV are just the tip of the iceberg. For every famous decorator or home flipper giving bad advice on TV, millions more can be found online in virtually every part of the world, including the designers operating just down the street from you that are either copying what they see on TV or practicing with little knowledge. It can be difficult to determine if they are qualified to do this work, yet people take their advice, pay them good money, and don't know enough about design themselves to discern if the final space will meet their needs.

Keep that in mind the next time you have an important project and need a professional's help. How can you know whether you can trust them? Do they ask about your problems and needs? Or do they ask about your tastes and style? If they're not asking you these kinds of questions, I recommend hanging up the phone and calling the next one until you find someone who seems to care about how you want to use and live in your space.

What makes all of this not just unfortunate but destructive is what happens next. People see images of visually striking but bad design shared in their social media feeds—designs they don't realize are flawed—and use that content to inform what they build. They don't think about whether the design solution will work for them in their space or for their lifestyle. Soon they are living in an environment based purely on style, not solutions. They judge spaces based on how good they look, not on how well the spaces serve them or others.

This is how design content lies to you: Much of what you see online is staged to look good in two-dimensional photographs and doesn't work well in your three-dimensional reality. There is no way to know if a space is functional by looking only at a photograph. When you look at pictures of architecture or interior design on your phone or computer, you get only a fraction of the felt experience. With social media, all you get is a freeze-frame of how something *looks*, nothing more.

None of us experiences the world like that.

We perceive the sounds of the environment, the textures of the materials, the color temperature of the lighting, the ergonomics of the furniture. It's a multisensory experience happening all at once. Each part of that experience affects the whole. You don't get that impression from a flat image. Can you tell from a photo of a library if it's a peaceful place to study, where the acoustics are good and noises from others won't bother you? Photos don't show you the full picture.

Much of what you see online is staged to look good in two-dimensional photographs and doesn't work well in your three-dimensional reality.

Perhaps the main reason we're unlikely to find great solutions on social media is that the best architectural solutions aren't necessarily the ones promoted by social media's algorithms. Anything that doesn't immediately get you hooked, even if it's the best architecture in the world, is replaced in the feed with something more exciting and trendier, and the good stuff rarely sees the light of day. It's best to be aware that social media is engineered to serve you content that keeps your brain engaged—not to improve your life with practical solutions to real problems.

In theory, social media could act as a positive force, amplifying incredible designs that change people's lives. It could spread useful information, educate people, and make everyone a better designer. But that's not the social media we've been given. The platforms we have today are run by companies whose business models incentivize them to maximize clicks and capital, not thoughtfulness. As a result, we all suffer—including future generations of architects, who are just now forming their opinions about design. They are internalizing the same skewed priorities the rest of us are exposed to on social media. What looks cool outshines what works well.

You might think you're safer relying on trusted publications for advice, but they're not necessarily better. Often, they're beholden to many of the same incentives as TV networks and social media platforms. For example, article headlines are often more sensational than factual: *This Glass House Redefines Luxury Living—But Would You Dare Live in It?* or *10 Stunning Homes That Prove Minimalism Is the Ultimate Flex*. They provoke you with emotional language paired with flashy imagery, and they'll include celebrity collaborations to draw your eye to a famous person's familiar face. None of this is nefarious on its own. What makes it devious is that almost none of the frivolous content is balanced with content focused on design solutions. The content appeals primarily to people's desire for beauty, social status, and perceptions of wealth. You can flip through an entire magazine and click and scroll until your hand is sore, and you may never find an article explaining *why* a design was created, other than that a famous person wanted it built.

Along the way, you may see a handful of trendy images of products the magazine or media outlet recommends for certain kinds of living, but even these are usually biased. In many cases, the outlet promoting the design typically has struck a deal with a retailer whose furniture or products are featured in the content, for which the outlet receives a cut of the profits when they sell something through their website or platform.

If it's pretty pictures you're after, then by all means, flip and scroll to your heart's content. But do so with the awareness that you are essentially walking into a candy store. You wouldn't buy your groceries there, so don't expect to find much nutritional value in the mansion tours or celebrity home stories. Scroll wisely.

HIGH-PRICED JUNK AND LIES

Here's an experiment: Pick your favorite design star and go to his or her website. Now find a product on their site and run an image search for that product. I'm willing to bet that the search results page shows dozens of identical products, all under different names, sold by different sites. No, those sites aren't reselling your favorite designer's product. That is the designer's product. Like every other seller who carries the item, the star designer found a product made cheaply overseas, called it something fancy sounding, and slapped his or her label on it with a hefty markup. Sound deceitful? It's actually a common practice in various industries known as "white labeling," and you'd be surprised how many of your favorite celebrity designers engage in the practice.

When I tell people that this is how name-brand designers make money, most people can't believe it. We're led to believe that these celebrities are talented designers who can solve our problems, but really they're talented marketers and salespeople who pawn off cheap products using their celebrity endorsement. I'm not saying these celebrity designers are illegitimate businesspeople. They're just not in the business people think they are. So how can we trust the design advice of a person who does this?

For the sake of argument, let's say you don't want to put your faith in the hands of a celebrity of TV or internet fame. Instead, you've hired a professional designer who came highly recommended. While this may sound like a safe bet, I know from experience that the products a professional recommends aren't necessarily the ones best suited to your goals or needs. Sometimes they're simply the products the designer can sell with the highest markups. When you buy them directly from the designer, the kickback to the designer is fatter than if you'd purchased a less expensive, although perhaps more appropriate, item. I don't have to tell you how deceitful this is. It would be like your doctor choosing not to prescribe you the medicine you need and, instead, prescribing whatever makes them the most money. In both cases, you are being denied access to greater well-being so that a trusted professional can turn a larger profit.

If that has you feeling disillusioned, I get it. You might be thinking, *What am I supposed to do? Who can I trust?*

Let me equip you with more insight, and then I'll offer several solutions to help you make educated, well-informed decisions for yourself and your spaces.

DEVELOPERS BUILD WHAT SELLS

Creators of design content aren't in the business of empowering you to become a better designer or exposing you to better ways of designing your spaces. Retailers, as a whole, aren't in the business of creating useful products to suit your needs. (You might be sensing a theme here.)

Each of these power brokers is focused on catering to the trends of the day and carefully tailoring their products to appeal to their target markets. You might say, *Well, isn't that what every business does?* No. The most admired and successful companies often keep the common good at the front of their business practices. They create things individuals want but in a way that preserves what broader society needs. This is what real estate developers should aspire to, but they often miss the mark.

Our third and final group of power brokers—real estate developers—are the companies that construct almost every building you see around you. In fact, they are largely responsible for *deciding* which buildings get built in the first place. Their job isn't just to negotiate the sale of homes, offices, and other buildings—it's to build the world we live in. They are the ones, more so than architects, city planners, and politicians, who decide what surrounds us physically.

For the most part, real estate companies treat development as a calculated business decision, not an opportunity to make life better. Your happiness and quality of life are not their priority. When they develop apartment towers, hallways are the minimum size allowed by code because they can't make money renting corridor space. Whether this makes it difficult for you to move in your furniture doesn't matter to them.

If you buy a house from a developer, the windows will probably be pushed to the edge of the building's exterior instead of recessed and will be built without overhangs or shutters for shade because that's cheaper to build and makes the space they're selling look as spacious as possible. They're not concerned that this will increase your heat exposure and energy bills. Their business model is about using the cheapest builder-grade materials and techniques acceptable, thinking about the environment only if there's a government incentive or tax break for them, and using poorly designed, flashy amenities to lure you to rent or buy.

Our world is currently being built by people who don't always have our best interests at heart. Explicitly or not, the power brokers in each of the three groups rely on one another to keep our world designed and us spending a certain way. They create the trends, reinforce the trends, and convince people to pour energy and money into re-creating those trends at home. These industry leaders could use their power for good—to teach people how to be smarter about their homes and spaces, to help us create better worlds for ourselves in which our spaces meet our real needs. Instead, we're at the mercy of profitability. Wherever the money goes, the machine of bad design follows.

What makes this so damaging is that architecture isn't some disposable thing. The tragedy of bad architecture is its permanence. Even the most carelessly designed buildings can stand for fifty to one hundred years. That's two or three generations of people forced to live with the frozen mistake of flawed architecture—and not just the people who *use* the building either. Every structure affects the people who live or work nearby, local ecological habitats, and future generations. Should the people in charge of this for society really be the ones incentivized to build whatever makes them more money?

Architecture isn't some disposable thing. The tragedy of bad architecture is its permanence.

Two million years ago, our primate ancestors built nests to serve their needs for deeper sleep. Fifteen thousand years ago, early humans built fences to serve their needs for controlled crops and livestock. And just a few hundred years ago, people built homes to serve the needs of their families and lifestyles. But we've lost our way.

The world we live in today offers unlimited exposure to trends from all over the world at every possible moment. We copy what we see, quickly and thoughtlessly, without an understanding of the consequences. And those in power take notice, selling us hollow trends that fill our homes.

Perhaps the problem was best summed up by design professor C. Thomas Mitchell: "A range of observers of architecture are now suggesting that the field may be bankrupt, the profession itself impotent, and the methods inapplicable to contemporary design tasks. . . . Collectively they are incapable of producing pleasant, livable, and humane environments, except perhaps occasionally and then only by chance."[2]

Our species has never been further from its architectural instincts than we are now. What we need is a smarter approach to design that addresses all the challenges we've been discussing and unlocks the life that awaits us. The problem is, such a philosophy has never been available to us.

Until now.

PART 2

THE SOLUTION

In this section, you'll learn the Baaham design philosophy. Whether you're redesigning your bedroom or building a skyscraper, Baaham principles give you the power to design around how people want to use the space, how people are wired to think and feel, and the broader context. Like a reference manual, this section can be revisited as often as necessary, until you feel you've mastered Baaham's principles.

4

THE POWER OF BAAHAM

A timeless philosophy can help us design our perfect world.

HUMANS AND OUR SPACES

Growing up, my first language wasn't English. It was Urdu, a language spoken throughout Pakistan, parts of India, the Middle East—and as far south as South Africa and as far north as Germany. A beautiful word from the Urdu language is *baaham,* meaning two things working together, in tandem, and influencing each other. The more places I design, the more I appreciate the word's meaning. It perfectly describes the relationship we have with our built environment. The spaces we're in aren't passive backgrounds to our lives; they are active participants, shaping who we become.

After decades of studying, analyzing, and creating aspects of the built world, I've concluded that the design philosophy the world needs is one rooted in this reciprocity between people and their spaces. The philosophy we need is Baaham.

Baaham, the design philosophy, didn't happen overnight. It didn't come to me in a dream or in a *eureka!* moment when an apple fell on my head. It was the culmination of decades spent trying to understand our relationship to our surroundings. And it all started in kindergarten when, one day, a boy peed on me.

I was five. Our classroom looked like any typical kindergarten: a patterned square rug where kids would plop down for story time, foldable vinyl mats for naptime, a colorful bookshelf stuffed with books of all shapes and sizes, and a rack of glazed ceramic mugs we were making for Mother's Day. There was also a bathroom attached to the back wall, and one afternoon, I really had to go.

It was a Jack and Jill bathroom—a single-occupancy bathroom with two doors connecting two classrooms: One door opened to my classroom, and one opened to another. The moment I realized this as I stepped into the room, another full-bladdered boy came bursting through the door, his pants already unbuttoned and pulled halfway down his legs.

What is happening?

He immediately began emptying his bladder. His urine sprayed wildly, landing all over the walls, the floor, and the toilet seat, but for the most part, right on me. I was trapped. The one-person room left me no choice but to try to duck out of his stream's path and wait until he finished.

By the time it was over, I was soaked. The front of my pants were drenched in this boy's pee, and now I had the humiliating task of rejoining my classmates, who had no idea what had just happened. Quietly, I took my seat on the rug, hoping no one would notice. But Mrs. Ray must have because she took me aside and fished out the unstylish acid-washed denim pants she reserved for kids who had accidents. Putting them on was humiliating. *Everyone probably thinks I peed my pants!*

As much as I wanted to blame that kid for what happened, he didn't know better. His physiology took over, and he used the space as it was intended. So did I. The real culprit was the awful design of that bathroom: joining two separate classrooms with one shared lavatory and expecting five-year-olds to navigate it correctly. Where else is that design acceptable? How was I, a child, supposed to know to lock *both* doors before using the restroom? And what would have happened if I had been doing more than just peeing?

I look back at that moment in kindergarten as the first time I can remember experiencing the power of design. As I grew older, I hung out in the back of my parents' dry-cleaning business and built whatever I could out of cardboard boxes, hanger wire, twist ties, pipe cleaners, buttons, safety pins, and any other spare materials I discovered in my orbit. I created houses, castles, robots, banjos, and buildings with moving contraptions like a Rube Goldberg machine.

It didn't matter what I built; I just liked the process of creating. It came naturally to me. I fell in love with buildings. On car rides, my face was glued to the window looking out at the world—something I still do today (if I'm not the one driving). But it wasn't until I was twelve that I got my first real taste of *designing* architecture.

My local mosque held a competition for students: Design a building that could win the Aga Khan Award for Architecture, a prize for buildings that address society's needs. My classmates jumped in. They designed hospitals, libraries, and cultural centers. I racked my brain. *What would make a difference for people?* Then I remembered.

The summer before third grade I had visited family in Pakistan. My first day there was an abrupt introduction to Karachi urban life with cows roaming, trash strewn about, and kids playing in the streets. My older cousin, Murad, and his friends—a crew of ten- and eleven-year-olds—played cricket. A lot of cricket. Every day, they were in the streets with tennis balls and makeshift wickets. Cars and rickshaws dangerously whizzed by, narrowly avoiding the kids. It was chaos. As I reflected on this, I knew what to design. Murad's neighborhood needed a recreation center! I grabbed a large sheet of twenty-four-by-thirty-six-inch graph paper, a ruler, and my finest pencils. For the next three days, I studied my design. I researched local species of banyan trees, drew cricket fields to scale, and created a place where Murad and his friends could play safely away from speeding rickshaws.

In the end, I lost the competition—to a hospital design for Uganda. I looked at my banyan trees and my community-centered cricket fields, and I was disappointed. But this feeling, and my ideas, were not lost. I had realized at a young age that I could use architecture to make people's lives better. The original drawing for the Karachi recreation center is still with me today, and it continues to serve as a reminder of architecture's power to serve people.

The older I got, however, the more I discovered that the architecture I wanted to make wasn't how things were typically done. As I began my career, I worked for world-renowned architects that had grown massive firms and won coveted Pritzker Architecture Prizes—true titans of the industry. I thought I would learn the ways of the masters, but what I got instead was a front-row seat to a design process that put flash over function, style over substance. These architects were supposed to be setting world-class examples for young minds, yet all I saw was a lame appeal to fleeting trends. Where were the people who would be using the space? Why didn't they have a seat at the table?

The older I got, the more I discovered that the architecture I wanted to make wasn't how things were typically done.

For these designers, an ongoing miseducation taught them to make things bold for the sake of publicity, to dial up the "curb appeal" and not dive deep into function. As a result, they created designs that looked sexy, for everyone to fawn over online, but were cold, lifeless places for occupants. Worse, the spaces might do real damage to human life or to the planet.

I felt disappointed and disillusioned. It seemed like the architecture world had forgotten the *why* behind design and had jumped right to the *what*. It placed too much emphasis on how to build without enough clarity on the purpose or process of designing the right buildings. But there was a silver lining. Many nights after work, a coworker and I would hole up in our office and work on side projects to submit to design competitions—like designing flood-resistant homes for cities ravaged by hurricanes. Sometimes we wouldn't leave until one or two in the morning, despite the seventy-hour workweeks we were already clocking (you know, the stuff we were actually paid for). The city would be sound asleep when I walked home, and I should have been exhausted, but that was when I felt most alive.

I knew that had to be my calling, not slogging away at a desk designing some random building to be "bold" for no other reason than boldness itself. So I quit. I decided to attend grad school, and soon after graduating,

I started my own design firm—one focused on creating spaces that uplift people and communities, especially those in disadvantaged positions. I made it my life's mission to show people how design can improve our world. To show them how the path to a healthy, prosperous life involves designing spaces that allow us and our surroundings to work together, in tandem, positively influencing each other.

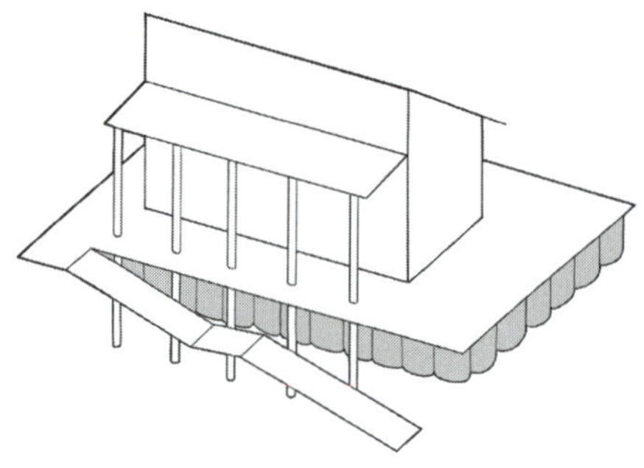

flood-resistant home

THE PRINCIPLES OF BAAHAM

That's where Baaham comes in. Baaham draws on the best ideas and practices from the past, such as vernacular construction, environmental psychology, human centered design, permaculture, and many others, and fuses them into a holistic, easy-to-follow philosophy. It's the result of working on hundreds of projects; reading thousands of pages on architectural theory, philosophy, and human behavior; and spending countless hours each day listening to people talk about their experiences in spaces and deeply observing my own experiences.

What I've learned is that design is about gaining deep understanding about oneself and others and the deploying that knowledge to give people new and better ways of living. While designing, we should keep in mind our ecosystem and watch for unintended consequences. From this insight, I've reflected on how to share the best parts of what I've learned so that you can design your world to improve your life and the lives of those around you. This book is your guide to reclaiming the power of your physical environment by using Baaham in whatever space you find yourself.

What follows are the principles of Baaham. These principles, when applied to any design project, ensure that you are maximizing the right outcomes for whoever that design will serve. It's not about promoting or criticizing a certain style or taste. Baaham is a process. It's a way of designing better spaces, no matter what style you prefer.

Look within

Put the people who predominantly use a space at the center of that space's design—their needs, goals, and aspirations—and then design outward.

Solve important problems

Prioritize solutions over appearances. Think practically about what people need from their space daily, and find form through function.

Design for change

Recognize the power of the built environment to nudge people toward desired behaviors and mindsets, and design so that the space can evolve over time as needs change.

Follow nature

Respect the influence that natural factors such as light, air, openness, and stimulation have on people. Use feedback to improve the design, just as organisms adapt to stay fit for their environments.

Embrace details
Pay close attention to the finer points of your design that affect how well the design functions, as well as the visual details that make people feel more comfortable in the space.

Build ecologically
Source materials and approaches to construction from the area in which you're building. Minimize the use of materials that do more harm than good to us and to the planet.

Zoom out
Pick design elements based on how they influence—and are influenced by—the other elements in the surrounding context. Consider unintended consequences.

At first glance, this may seem like a random grouping of principles, but it's not. It's a carefully organized system. In the following chapters, let's take a closer look at how these principles play out in the world around you.

5

LOOK WITHIN

Every great design serves someone's needs.

FIND YOUR TARGET

In any successful design project, an important reflection needs to happen, whether you're designing for others or for yourself. The designer must understand the needs of the people for whom he or she is designing. That's *why* the design project exists: because someone has a need. By uncovering those needs, you can establish a goal for the design—what the design wants to achieve. Without this deep reflection, you won't have a target to aim for. The design you create may be aesthetically pleasing, but it won't work the way it should or serve people in the most supportive ways.

We should remember that design affords us the opportunity to push our cities and homes one step closer to the kinds of places in which we want to live—and push us to become the kinds of people we hope to be. We must take that opportunity seriously. We should think deeply about what a good life looks like and what kinds of experiences we want to have. That vision becomes our target.

Looking within requires depth. It's not an exercise in determining someone's style or artistic taste. It's a deep, introspective process of observation, reflection, and inquiry to bring to light all the hidden needs, desires, challenges, and opportunities from using a particular space—and not just for one person but for anyone who uses the space or may be affected by it.

HOW TO LOOK WITHIN

To begin looking within, you first need to know who exactly you're learning more about. This is the person or group of people who will be most affected and influenced by the design. If you're designing a new apartment where you'll be living alone, that person is you. But for every project, you should also keep in mind the people whose needs might not be so obvious.

We should think deeply about what a good life looks like and what kinds of experiences we want to have. That vision becomes our target.

For example, if you're designing an office, you need to consider not only the core employees, but also the IT staff, the custodial staff, and any visitors who will need to navigate the space. In a grocery store, the people to keep in mind are not just the shoppers, but also the cashiers and staff in charge of stocking shelves, loading and unloading trucks, and retrieving shopping carts. To properly look within, you must identify who primarily uses the space *and* the many secondary stakeholders whose experiences and needs also matter.

Let's say you're not the designer. Let's say you're a city official in charge of green-lighting a large urban development project. You might think, *It's not my responsibility to look within. That's why I hire architects.* But that's only half right.

It's the architect's job to thoroughly examine how the project will affect people, but it's also your job as the person in power—the one overseeing the project from a greater vantage point—to do your due diligence and determine who the project affects beyond the people using the space. If you're building affordable housing or a new city park, more people than just the dwellers in the housing unit or future park-goers will be affected. Those who work near the housing unit and businesses currently located by the park will also be affected. It's up to you to figure out who will be indirectly affected by the design and take their needs and quality of life into consideration as well.

Once you've identified who the design will impact most, it's time to start getting to know these people better. You should do this both by observing them as well as engaging with them. The goal is to understand:

- What context are they coming from and situated in?
- What are their needs (even needs they can't immediately articulate)?
- How do they relate to the space, and how do others use that space?
- What are their pains and frictions?
- What are their aspirations for how they want to live?

It's tempting to be influenced by what others have, by trends and styles, and by the idea that what you see online, on TV, or in magazines is what's best for a person. Looking within means ignoring those trends so you can reflect on true needs and on what will serve the people who use the space. These priorities are foundational to Baaham, and with the right steps, anyone can master them.

Mindshift: Become aware of your own experiences in space

Before you design anything, think about your relationship to space. This awareness is the foundation for becoming a great designer.

If you're sitting at your desk and are suddenly blinded by the afternoon sun, think about whether poor design could be the culprit. Is the layout of your office doing you a disservice? Do you need shading for when the sun crosses your window?

Before you design anything, think about your relationship to space. This awareness is the foundation for becoming a great designer.

This introspection doesn't always come naturally. Sometimes we want to use the space for whatever it is we have going on at that moment. But during the design process, we must bring a new level of thoughtfulness to our experiences. Stop and think about your relationship to the space. Pay attention to the layout: How easy is it to move around? Does the noise level feel comfortable or disruptive? Is the lighting appropriately bright, dim, warm, or cool? The more you can feel firsthand how spaces affect you, the better designer you'll be.

Mindshift: Observe like a sociologist

An insight I learned from my art classes is that many artists struggle with drawing because they haven't learned to look closely. Because they can't see well, they don't draw well. Often, we design buildings the same way—without looking closely at how people behave and operate, what they need, how they interact, and how they relate to spaces.

Start conducting sociological "studies" of places you visit, observing how people move through the space. If you're designing a hospital, for example, your study might include how easily nurses, doctors, and other staff move through the hallways and how often they bump into one another during surgery in the operating room. Your study might also include observations of how easily visiting family members can get where they need to go and whether the noise levels in the hospital affect communication between patients and their doctors.

As you conduct these exercises, play the role of silent observer. You're not intervening or interfering. What you're looking for is when people struggle, when things go wrong, and how the design of the space could be playing a role. You want to keep your eyes and ears open to notice the invisible forces of design influencing people toward certain behaviors.

Practice: Host workshops

One way I engage with stakeholders is through workshops. I involve them in my process so they can share pains and frictions with me directly. You can do this too.

Before sitting down with the people who will use the space, ask yourself, *What do I need to learn about them? What information will make it possible for me to design something for them?* When you do sit down with them, avoid the temptation to ask, "What styles do you like?" or, "How do you want it to look?" and instead ask, "What experience do you want to have?"

Asking the right questions will help you create a more effective design.

For example, if you're designing a school building, gather a group of students, preferably in a classroom so they can look around and refer to things, and ask, "What makes it hard for you to focus or learn at school?" Then give them drawing supplies and let them sketch ideas for how they might change the room so they can focus better. Get to the root of what the people you're designing for are saying.

If you're redesigning your home, gather everyone in the living room, and host the workshop there. Ask your family what they want out of the space, and watch them get excited as they start to become part of the process.

Throughout the workshops, remind the people you're designing for that their problem is not that they need a new space or building. Their problem is that they want something to happen—they want to accommodate X or they want people to do Y or they want result Z to occur. So if I'm your designer, I'm not going to ask you to tell me about the building you need. That's not your problem. I'm going to ask you about what you're trying to achieve.

Once, when I designed an after-school technology lab in Oakland, California, I discovered through initial workshops that the people organizing the program had five goals for the space:

1. Connect students to resources by building a place-based program in their neighborhood.
2. Assure students of color, primarily Black and Hispanic teens, that they belong in the tech field.

3. Increase the appeal of computer science professions.
4. Build student confidence and risk-taking.
5. Instill in students a maker mindset.

These five goals served as our target. Anytime a staff member asked if we could create a specific kind of environment, I could ask, "How do you see that serving our objectives?" This is true for the ideas that clients will have as well as for your ideas. In a good design, each decision will point back to the objectives of the project. This includes which property or site you develop, the material you select for a countertop, and dozens of other decisions big and small. Having these objectives for the Oakland project ensured that any design we arrived at solved *their* problem—nothing came into existence just because someone thought it would be cool or interesting.

These workshops are often revealing. Listening to people's stories and ideas will give you insights into their lived experiences and what about those experiences the design should be working to change and improve. In addition, through this exercise, people often initially think they want one thing but then realize they need something different; they simply couldn't see it before.

When I've conducted these workshops, I've challenged people's assumptions that they need hallways or classrooms. They might come to me saying they need eight new classrooms, but through the principle of *look within*, I learn what they actually need are fewer classrooms but more nooks for quiet reflection or multipurpose spaces for group activities.

Practice: Tour different spaces to find your sweet spot

One challenge with looking within is knowing how to articulate how well a space works for you. You can expand your vocabulary by visiting different versions of the same space.

For example, if you're redesigning your bathroom, you may struggle to answer how you'd like it to work. Isn't it just a bathroom? You'd be surprised. If I took you to your friend's house to use their bathroom, then to the local library to use its bathroom, and finally to an expensive hotel to use its bathroom, you'd come away with three very different experiences.

More important, you'd be able to tell me what about each bathroom you liked and didn't like—which one felt most comfortable, which one had the most convenient faucet for washing your hands, and which one generally made it easiest for you to handle your business. You can do this exercise for yourself or for the people you're designing for.

In both cases, finding a range of experiences to compare creates a more holistic understanding of what the design needs to accomplish for the people using the space.

Mindshift: Keep an open mind

At the beginning of a project, it might be that all you want to do is bring your design to life. Maybe you've thought about this project for months or years, and you've been saving up to afford this transformation. When the time finally comes, you have all these ideas in your head of how you want the space to look. You can see it perfectly.

But let's tap the brakes for a second.

Until you've done a thorough investigation of your needs, experiences, and aspirations, you won't be able to say whether the design you have in mind is the right one for you (or whoever you're designing for). There may be elements that make sense, but without looking within, it's unlikely the design will fit you well.

Hard as it may be, early in the design phase, we must drop any preconceived notions about what the design ought to look like and follow the process. I promise you'll end up someplace even better than you imagined.

PUTTING IDEAS INTO PRACTICE

A heartfelt example of *look within* is the David H. Koch Center for Cancer Care at New York City's Memorial Sloan Kettering Cancer Center. During the creation process, the designers recognized that cancer patients often feel like time is out of their control, so they decided the facility needed to give back a sense of control in life-affirming ways.

In addition to hundreds of exam and procedure rooms, the twenty-five-floor Center for Cancer Care includes three distinct floor types: restoration, recreation, and activation. These floors are repeated in sets of three throughout the building so patients are always within a few floors of each one. On restoration floors, patients can spend time in small libraries, meditation huts, and intimate seating areas for private conversation. Or patients can choose to go to recreation floors and visit cafés, social kitchens, and exercise classes. Or to an activation floor, where they can find open spaces for socializing, with games, puzzles, and other activities. When patients visit these floors, they don't have to worry about missing an appointment because a personalized "real time location system" will notify them when it's time to come back, removing the need to wait around in their respective patient rooms for a nurse.

This way of thinking about the patient and visitor experience exemplifies looking within, and it marks an important step toward addressing some of the greatest psychological needs patients and their loved ones face during a worrisome hospital stay.

Look within is an essential tool in your design process. The designer should help the people who will be using the space refine their request for what they want to build—because even though everyone might know what a house is and can recall a house they liked, it might not be exactly what they *need*. It's up to the designer to interrogate and find out precisely what the person is looking for, what their life is like, what they and their family like to do.

It is the designer's responsibility to help them refine what they're asking for by looking within.

To start looking within, ask yourself: *Who am I designing for, and what do they need from their space?*

6

SOLVE IMPORTANT PROBLEMS

When designing, pick the right problems. Then prioritize solutions that make life better.

TWO LEVELS OF PROBLEM-SOLVING

Every project presents an opportunity to choose which problems are important and worth solving. We can do this in two ways: first, by picking which projects to work on, and second, by choosing which objectives matter for the project.

In this endeavor, it's easy to lose focus or to waste energy solving an unimportant problem. Solving an important problem, for example, would be designing your home so that you and your family enjoy it. Getting distracted by an unimportant problem would be designing it around resale value, since that may not give you and your family what you need while you're living there. Are you willing to sacrifice your comfort and happiness for the next ten, twenty, or thirty years because you're trying to solve for the fickle and unpredictable desires of a perfect stranger, just because they might buy your home one day?

If we shift our thinking from the superficial to a respect for the way architecture influences our lives, we can use design as a tool to solve problems and build the kind of world we want to live in.

The first opportunity is choosing which projects are worth our attention. To do that, we need to understand which problems matter. We need to listen to the needs of our communities, understand the challenges they face, and work to develop solutions that meet their needs.

The stakes couldn't be higher.

Communicable diseases spread in hospitals, yet changes in design and protocols can save lives. Kids living in noisier homes are slower to develop reading skills, yet design tailored for focus and concentration can speed up their ability to learn.[1] Most American cities don't have walkable streets because they are dominated by cars, yet walkable streets make us happier, healthier, and more productive and creative.[2]

These problems of health and performance outcomes are partly because of poor design—and it's up to us to stop solving the unimportant "problems" and start focusing on what's important instead. State and city officials: Are you funding projects that make the world better? If you're a professional designer, do you view design as a tool for making life better? For young designers, especially, it will be tempting to take on any project that comes your way. You may think you don't have the power yet to question what we build, but you do. You're a member of your community and a human on this planet. You have impact. Don't build things you don't believe are right. As a society, what we choose to build reflects what we value. We must choose with intention.

An example of solving unimportant problems can be found in Dubai. In the 1980s and '90s, when the United Arab Emirates looked at the West and decided it wanted to prove that it too had the means to build skyscrapers—that it was no less of a nation, that it could build the symbols of a booming economy—the city of Dubai began building soaring glass towers in the desert, which makes little sense for that climate. Dubai didn't solve for the important problems, like how to keep people cool and comfortable in the extreme heat. It focused on impressing others. In doing so, the city amplified environmental problems that extended far beyond its borders: sand shortages from building artificial islands, the burning of fossil fuels to cool glass towers in the desert, and all the costs associated with extracting and transporting the materials used in construction.

What we choose to build reflects what we value. We must choose with intention.

If you feel you must commit to a project that doesn't add clear value for humanity and is more focused on competition or profits, then you need to ask, *At what cost?* Each project requires or produces some level of extraction, emissions, waste, and materials. By taking on these projects, what are the social and environmental costs to our communities? What important things are we *not* able to build because of these decisions?

We shouldn't build just anything. Everything should be *worth* building.

+ + +

Beyond picking the right projects to work on, the second way to *solve important problems* is choosing which objectives to focus on. Knowing your desired outcomes allows you to achieve the goals that are most meaningful to you. Remember: The word *design* comes from the Latin *designare*, meaning "to contrive" or "plot." Whenever you're designing a space or having it designed, you should be asking, *What is the point of the space? What do I want it to achieve?*

For example, if you're designing your bedroom, ask yourself, *What is the point of my bedroom?* Your answer might be that the purpose of your bedroom is to rest. That's it. It's easy, though, to get distracted and focus on solving less important problems, like how much your bedroom might impress friends who visit. Or maybe the style feels dated, and you don't want people to think you're out of touch. Or you saw a new design trend online that caught your eye. But what *problems* are you solving when you implement these things? If you're redecorating a space at home, use that as an opportunity to solve important problems. Don't simply redecorate or refresh a space; *redesign* it.

Whenever you're designing a space or having it designed, you should be asking, *What is the point of the space?*

Solve important problems is about going deeper than appearances. It's about recognizing that form has a function. Form dictates how a space and people function. Because form affects our experience in this way and is not purely decorative, it should be created with a purpose in mind—the problem it's trying to solve.

An example of solving important problems is the traditional house of Malaysia, which locals conceived to meet their needs and respond to the surrounding climate. Each house features a roof made from natural materials, like thatch, that prevent heat from radiating into the house; the house

is raised on stilts to afford dwellers privacy, catch cooling winds, protect against floods, and offer storage space in drier months; and prefabricated parts allow families to expand the house if they welcome new members into the home.[3]

The Malay house is a great example of how addressing the important problems in design can create meaningful outcomes that affect people's well-being and the functionality of the space. Solving important problems is also about measuring what really matters in a design—not focusing on superficial metrics that designers or building owners will sometimes boast about, like how colossal the building is or how far a slab of marble traveled to reach its destination.

In some cases, people are now flipping that metric and saying, "Look at how *little* material we used," which is a positive shift and possibly a result of environmental and sustainable development initiatives and mandates. Still, other factors relating to the success of the project tend not to get measured, such as how happy the occupants of the building are and if the design met their objectives (e.g., better family life, more productivity at work, enhanced learning, healthier patients, etc.). As the saying goes, what gets measured gets improved. And since these human outcomes aren't measured, we're not improving them. We're not focusing on them. We're eyeing problems that aren't all that important, partly because they're easy to measure—like how tall a building is—instead of what really matters.

HOW TO SOLVE IMPORTANT PROBLEMS

I rely on a few techniques to implement this principle. They are meant to clarify the problems you'll be solving and help focus your time, energy, and resources on the problems that matter most. I encourage you to revisit these techniques as you move through a project to check that the problems you are currently solving are still the ones you ought to be solving.

Practice: Conduct a strengths-challenges analysis

Even for existing spaces, *solve important problems* can help you ensure that the next redesign doesn't become just a redecoration—a visual refresh instead of a chance to solve actual problems. The best approach I've found in these situations is conducting a strengths-challenges analysis. This is where you identify how the current space meets your priorities and where it falls short. By being a close and analytical observer, you can map out how the current environment is either helping or hurting the causes you care about and then redesign it to meet those objectives.

Let's say you're redesigning your living room, and you want this space to be optimized for throwing parties and entertaining, rather than just sitting and watching TV. When you conduct your strengths-challenges analysis, take these objectives into account. You may realize, for instance, that you need darker or patterned fabrics that won't show stains as easily; or that by ditching the chaise leg of your sofa, you can bring in two extra seats; or that lightweight furnishings make it easier to rearrange the room for different types of social gatherings, so a heavy coffee table might not suit your goals. These are the kinds of challenges you'll want to identify in your analysis.

On the other hand, you may realize that certain elements, such as the acoustics or technology in the space, already lend themselves well to social gatherings. Recognizing where your design meets or falls short of your objectives allows you to home in on how your space currently works for you and where problems exist that still need solving.

Mindshift: Slow down

Speed can cause us to lose sight of what matters. We get ahead of ourselves and start thinking about tiny things before the big, important things. Create a reflective environment and invite everyone involved to ask, "Is the design headed in the right direction? Is it meeting the goals we've laid out? Is this still worth doing, or have we lost our way?"

Too many designers and developers rush the design process. Recently, I worked on a project in a small Midwestern city as a consultant, and the design team was being pressured by the client's project manager to meet extremely fast targets that couldn't possibly allow for the development of good architecture. Design a sixteen-thousand-square-foot learning center in fourteen days? There's no way a good design fit can be achieved that fast.

When you start a project, study the problem and context. For the first week, don't draw anything. Spend your time thinking and discussing, because the first idea you have may be more about you (your personal preference) than about what the project needs. By waiting to begin drawing, you'll save yourself from this. The design can then be based on a deep consideration of the problem.

Mindshift: Question the status quo

The way something is designed isn't necessarily the best it'll ever be. That's just the latest best solution someone came up with. Everything was designed, so it can always be redesigned. Let all possible solutions be up for grabs. By ignoring how things are typically designed, you open yourself to designing something new and possibly better.

In cities like New York, for example, it can be difficult for public buses to make tight turns. So a group of designers figured out that if you cut the bus in half and rejoin it with an accordion-like connector, the bus is flexible in the middle and can make sharp turns more easily. This design challenged the assumption that buses must be built as one rigid tube and, instead, put the needs of the bus first.

Someday, another designer may come along and improve this design even more. It's not perfect or finished. It's merely the latest best design our society has come up with.

Mindshift: Go deep, not shallow

With the right objectives, you can help your design the most by devising solutions at a deep level versus a superficial or shallow level.

For example, if you're designing your home office, you might have a vague sense that you want the design to be *amazing* without really asking yourself what it means for the space to be amazing. Staying superficial would mean you don't question it, so you default to making a space that's visually striking or lavish, perhaps based on the latest images you've found while scrolling social media.

But really, you should consider what would make it amazing to *use*, whether that's for creative brainstorming or focused work. What would create an amazing experience?

Don't get stuck in the superficial. Dig deeper to see what lies beneath. Ask yourself questions such as:

- *What do I need to achieve when in this office?*
- *What makes it hard for me to focus or get work done?*
- *What physiological needs (e.g., temperature, light, physical comfort) most affect how I perform?*

PUTTING IDEAS INTO PRACTICE

A thoughtful example of *solve important problems* can be found in Malmö, Sweden, a city that thought deeply about how to make it easier and more pleasurable for commuters to get around, which makes for healthier and more well-connected citizens.

For one, the city recognized that taking the bus is fraught with uncertainty: *Will the bus get here on time? Will I be late to where I'm going?* To solve this uncertainty, bus stops in Malmö now feature countdown timers with extra-large numbers that show the number of minutes until the next bus arrives. From far away, people can read the signs and know whether they need to run to catch the bus or if they have enough time to walk there leisurely.

In addition, the railway station was designed with a clever feature that helps solve "last mile" problems getting around the city. A typical last mile problem in many cities is that you can take a bus or train nearly all the way to your destination, but then you must walk or bike the last bit. Now the railway stations in Malmö have convenient tracks running up the side of the stairs for people to easily wheel their bikes up the steps.[4] Back at street level, they can just hop on and cycle to their destinations. Without the track, people are less incentivized to lug their bikes up and down the stairs. But with it, commuters can get where they need to go relatively hassle-free.

By thinking through what was important, the city of Malmö was able to design an urban experience that improves the quality of life for residents.

+ + +

Ultimately, solving important problems is an exercise in narrowing our focus. There are infinite problems we can identify and rationalize as important, but most of these so-called problems disappear if we're ruthless about articulating what *really* matters.

If you're ever in doubt about what's an important problem, ask yourself if solving the problem contributes to a better standard of living for the people using the space. If it doesn't—if it puts money, status, or aesthetics over experience—chances are it's not an important problem.

Through this lens, it's easy to see what constitutes an important problem. The difficult part is admitting to yourself, either as the designer or the person using the space, that unimportant problems don't matter. But once you do, I promise you'll notice an immediate shift in your ability to identify what truly matters and to create life-changing designs.

To start solving important problems, ask yourself: *What's the most important goal this space needs to achieve?*

7

DESIGN FOR CHANGE

Our environments change us and ought to change themselves.

TWO KINDS OF CHANGE

People want certain things when they build a new space. Then they move in, start living and working there, and over time their needs evolve. This happens on an individual level with people's needs changing over time and at a societal level as our cultures continue to evolve. *Design for change* has two meanings, each reflecting a way our designs ought to facilitate change.

The first meaning refers to design's ability to change us as people—to nudge us toward the behaviors, feelings, and mindsets we most desire and away from the ones we wish to avoid. (This isn't to be confused with social engineering, which, by definition, is a form of manipulation that often violates people's real interests.) When it comes to improving people's lives, how often do we stop to consider design's influence on our psyches and relationships, if it ever occurs to us at all? Everywhere we go, we are changed and influenced in some way by the designs that surround us, such that over time, our lives unfold within—and are directed by—the structures we make. We literally become products of our environments.

As designers, each time we place a brick, we are impacting someone's life. We need to be aware of the power of the built environment and create the right experiences for people—for example, to help people develop good habits in their homes, to create feelings of community within neighborhoods, and to instill a creative mindset at schools and in offices.

How often do we stop to consider design's influence on our psyches and relationships?

The second meaning refers to how the design itself should be adaptable because people's needs change over time. Society changes in the ways it works, learns, and plays, so the designs that serve communities must evolve to support those changing ways of life. If change is the only constant, then we should never assume that a design can be static, locking people into a certain way of living.

When places are designed with change in mind, not only do they better serve the needs of the people using them over time; they are also more sustainable. Adaptable designs can be updated and reused without much hassle or waste, rather than being demolished and rebuilt from the ground up.

Mastering both aspects of this principle of Baaham will allow you to create spaces that help people become who they most want to be while the spaces themselves evolve to meet society's changing needs.

NUDGES

Speaking to the British Parliament in 1943, Winston Churchill said, "We shape our buildings and afterwards our buildings shape us."[1] He was repeating an idea he'd brought up two decades prior at the Architectural Association awards ceremony when he said, "There is no doubt whatever about the influence of architecture and structure upon human character and action. We make our buildings and afterwards they make us. They regulate the course of our lives."[2]

In both instances, Churchill was referring to design's power to nudge us in certain directions over others. At their best, buildings do more than just shelter us—they remind us of what we find important and who we want to be. They guide us toward positive behaviors, thoughts, emotions, and, ultimately, identities.

Let me offer a handful of examples of how architectural nudges show up in our built environment so you can see the true scale of their influence.

At **school**, students have been shown to form a higher perception of themselves when the school buildings themselves are of a higher quality, that is, buildings that are made of quality materials, let in more sunlight, have better ventilation, are cleaner, and are better maintained overall. Researchers who study these effects have determined that a school's quality seems to communicate to students whether they deserve a nice learning environment.[3] In the "good" buildings, students think more highly of themselves. In the "bad" buildings, they are more likely to have a lower self-perception. The quality of the building, therefore, acts as a nudge for students, guiding them toward either positive or negative self-beliefs.

Students also take cues from their learning environments in terms of what kinds of attitudes and behaviors they're inclined to adopt. For example, learning environments with too many posters, graphics, drawings, and displayed projects tend to inhibit students' focus and absorption.[4] Basically, they're distracting. If the walls are cluttered and visually "noisy," students will have a harder time concentrating on the work in front of them.[5]

At **grocery stores**, the layout influences how shoppers navigate the aisles, how long they spend in the store, and, ultimately, what they buy. For instance, have you ever noticed that produce is usually positioned near the entrance? That's because once you've picked up some healthy foods, you're more likely to give yourself license to grab unhealthy snacks as well, which means the grocery store sells more. Or have you noticed that some of the most common staples like bread and milk are at the back of the store? That is intentional. In part, it's so the dairy items can be easily unloaded from a refrigerated truck into the store's refrigerators, but it's also designed this way because it forces you to walk past all the many other items in order to buy your eggs and milk.[6] And once you get to the back of the store, typically the dairy aisle is perpendicular to the rest of the aisles. That is also intentional. It forces you to see the other aisles, nudging you to think of other foods you might like to buy.

Add to all of this that many grocery stores place products that generate the highest profit margins on endcaps or right at shoppers' eye levels (because people are more likely to pick up products that are displayed at eye level), provide large shopping carts that silently communicate *Fill me up*, and lay out the store in various labyrinthian ways, making shoppers pass every aisle in the store. Few if any aspects of today's shopping experience aren't deliberately designed to nudge people toward buying more.

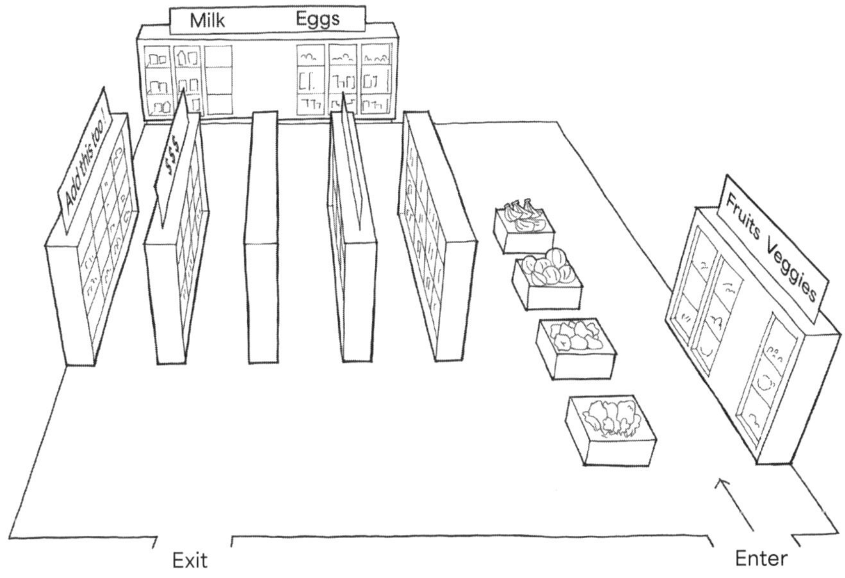

At **work**, the design of corporate offices influences the way employees think, how they interact with one another, and how well they can do their jobs. For example, people tend to have more serendipitous meetings in horizontal buildings rather than vertical ones. In vertical buildings, you don't typically have a reason to visit floors that aren't your own. In a horizontal building, however, you may walk down the hall to get to an amenity or a staircase or an exit.

An example of this is MIT's Building 20 in Cambridge, Massachusetts. The building is laid out in five low wings. People who have used the building for decades say the layout encourages interaction between people working on separate projects. One person who spent their career there observed that "in a vertical layout with small floor areas, there is less research variety on each floor. Chance meetings in an elevator tend to terminate in the lobby, whereas chance meetings in a corridor tended to lead to technical discussions."[7]

In my experience, it seems even the nature of discussions is different when you run into someone in the elevator lobby of a tall building—maybe you make small talk—versus in the hallway of a horizontal building, where maybe you pause for longer and have a wall surface to sketch on or a table to sit around and share ideas. This was the intent behind Steve Jobs's design of the Pixar headquarters in 1986. Rather than put the office's cafeteria, mailboxes, café, gift shop, and bathrooms along the sides of the building, Jobs had them installed in a central atrium to encourage chance run-ins between colleagues from different divisions. The building itself nudged people to become more social and spark new ideas. According to employees, the approach worked. Spontaneous meetings and information sharing increased.[8]

The design of an office also affects the way individuals think. Research shows, for instance, that people tend to be more creative under taller ceilings and more focused under shorter ones.[9] Have you ever noticed that yourself? A low ceiling guides your head down to the task at hand. It keeps your gaze on your work, similar to how blinders on a racehorse keep it focused. Because it's a smaller space (lower ceiling = less spatial volume), there's less room for distractions. A high ceiling, or expansive space, lifts this weight off you. You can look up. You feel more open. You can dream and wonder. You're not just looking down at your work. You're free to gaze up and ponder new connections between different ideas.

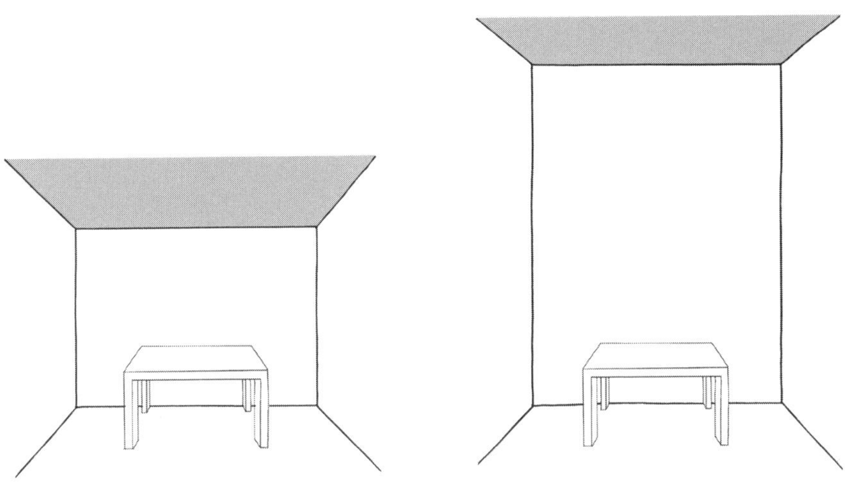

Maybe you're able to go for a walk outside. I've noticed this myself many times; my mind will make connections and surprise me with far-out thoughts and curiosities, all because of the openness outdoors.

Similarly, offices with open-plan seating, where a lot of employees are grouped into one big room, may help some colleagues brainstorm, but it may also create distractions, impeding others' ability to focus. Since companies want employees to be both creative and focused, designers should aim to create environments that allow for both.

At **home**, we may adopt certain habits that improve (or worsen) our health based on the ways we're nudged to behave there—and often, subtle changes can have a major impact on your everyday well-being. One example is the height of your bed, which affects how much you're required to use your joints and muscles. In a typical Western bedroom, a high bed on a box spring requires almost no effort to get in and out of. A person can easily sit or fall onto the bed and swing into a comfortable position. In traditional Japanese homes, however, beds are built low to the ground. A benefit to this design is that people must use their muscles and joints to lower themselves into the bed at night and to get up from the floor in the morning. Over the years, these thousands of repetitions preserve their health and keep them more physically capable. People who spend a lifetime sleeping in high Western beds may not enjoy those late-in-life abilities because their bed never required (nudged) them to use their muscles in those ways.

Other rooms of the home also nudge people toward healthier behaviors. In the kitchen, where people store certain foods can influence how much they make that particular food part of their diet. For instance, if you don't eat enough fruit or nuts, placing them in a highly visible spot in your kitchen, either at eye level or in places where they're easy to grab, will increase the chances that you snack healthfully.

The same is true with staying hydrated. Not long ago, I decided I wanted to drink water when I first woke up. I use my phone as my alarm and keep it on a shelf in my office instead of in the bedroom so I'm forced to get out of bed to turn it off (it also stops me from checking messages at night). I decided the best spot for my water bottle was next to my phone. That way, I can turn off my alarm and chug twelve ounces of water first thing in the morning. Making a spot for the water has built this habit. But when I travel and don't have that dedicated spot, I'm far less likely to practice this healthy behavior. The way I've designed this aspect of my personal space allows me to be healthier without having to think too hard. It's just the default now.

A final example from home: In the house where I grew up, my bathroom was furthest from the water heater in the garage. It took three minutes to get hot water in my sink. I didn't want to waste that much water waiting for the water to eventually turn hot, so I just wouldn't wash my face before bed. The layout of my house affected my personal habits. Without realizing it at the time, I was being nudged toward behaviors that probably led to more clogged pores and skin breakouts because the design obstructed my goal.

Design offers no shortage of ways to create nudges. You can adjust the layout, aesthetics, acoustics, lighting, materials, graphics, walls, floors, technology, and more. How you make use of these tools to nudge people is what will determine whether the design is effective at achieving its goals.

Make no mistake: No design is passive. Our spaces are always influencing us in some way. Building without an eye toward people's desired outcomes means you could unintentionally be nudging them in unhelpful directions, creating negative experiences, and guiding the course of their lives in ways they never wanted. It's essential to create environments that move people closer to their goals, not farther away from them.

Designs that nudge people toward their desired behaviors are powerful because they take effort off the individual. They make the most desirable actions easier to perform and the most desirable thoughts and feelings more likely to surface because the barriers to all of them are reduced. Good design makes it easier to become the people we most want to be.

HOW TO NUDGE PEOPLE

Creating the right nudges in a design requires a baseline awareness of how our environments influence us, plus a more specific understanding of what's getting in the way of people achieving their intended thoughts, feelings, or behaviors. With this information, it then falls on designers to open their tool kits and begin brainstorming the nudges that will work best for overcoming the obstacles at hand.

Mindshift: Build awareness of how environments nudge us

Great designers are great observers.

What about each space's layout, aesthetics, volume, lighting, acoustics, and materials affects the way you feel and think in the space? Do you feel compelled to behave in a certain way? Do you feel more or less social? Creative? Energized? Calm? Being an observer of yourself will help you better observe others, even as you enter spaces unfamiliar to you. In turn, you'll develop an intuition for how people's surroundings are influencing them.

For example, the next time you're in an airport and walk up to your gate, notice how the seats are arranged. At many airports, seating is laid out in what's known as a *sociofugal* arrangement, meaning it discourages social interaction. The chairs are usually in rows. Sometimes the rows all face the same direction so that, when you sit, you're facing the back of others' heads instead of facing them. And if you sat next to someone you don't know, you're unlikely to chat because you're not making eye contact and you're both facing forward.

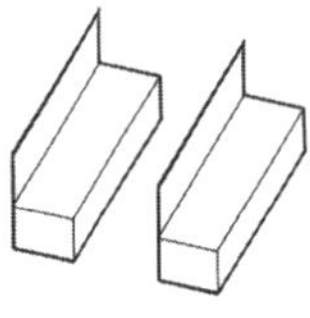

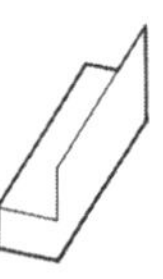

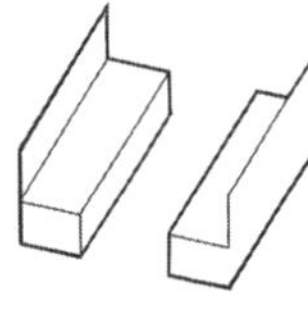

sociopetal

Other times, the rows face one another. This is known as a *sociopetal* layout, meaning it's more likely to encourage social interaction, but it's still sociofugal because the row facing you is generally too far from you—wide enough for people to pass with their luggage—to comfortably initiate or hold a conversation. You'd feel like you were yelling or disturbing others because of the gap between the rows or like your conversation couldn't be private.

The next time you're waiting for a flight, ask yourself, *How might the airport experience change if the seats were rearranged? How might I be nudged to behave or think differently based on a different layout of the seating?*

Sometimes what you'll notice is that a design changes how you think about yourself. If you've ever attended a concert in a big arena, you've likely realized that the lighting focuses entirely on the performers onstage. The audience usually stays unlit. This one design decision—putting a spotlight on the performers and shrouding the audience in darkness—sends the message that the performers are what's important. The audience members, not so much. In the crowd, you're part of the throng of fans, so you may be more likely to think of yourself as an audience member rather than a unique individual.

Whether accidental or intentional, the design of our environments influences us wherever we go. And once you start looking for these influences, they become nearly impossible to miss.

Practice: Understand obstacles to the desired behavior

With an awareness of how our buildings shape us, you can begin to scan the environment of the people you're designing for in search of obstacles that may be standing between them and their desired goals.

For example, if a family tells me that they feel like they're not spending enough quality time together at home, I can quantify how much the design of their home is playing a role in that experience. I can measure what percentage of their home is designed for spending quality time together—for instance, through the number of social spaces and places for communal gathering—and what percentage is discouraging those sorts of interactions. If only a tiny percentage of the home allows for this type of interaction, it may be a sign that we need to increase the amount of space allocated to that.

Practice: Understand people's context and conditioning

Interviewing the people who use the space, engaging them deeply, and getting them to design solutions with you will also illuminate any prior conditioning they may be bringing to how they ought to behave in the space. Often, past conditioning blinds us to obstacles that stand in the way of our desired behaviors.

For example, let's say we're designing a school, and the administration asks us to create a place that encourages teachers to collaborate. In talking to a teacher about what might get in the way of that goal, we realize they've been conditioned to think that each teacher "owns" his or her classroom. They believe the classroom is where they ought to teach, take their breaks, plan their lessons, and even eat their lunches, often because that's what they saw other teachers doing, or it's how they were taught, or the scheduling never allowed time for socializing with other teachers. As a result, they've been conditioned not to spend much time in communal spaces such as a lounge or break room, where they might interact with colleagues.

By understanding the person or people we are designing for and where they're coming from, we're able to design solutions that can be more effective. It's similar to the way doctors can better diagnose patients and design treatment protocols if they know more about a patient's context and lifestyle, rather than crafting treatments based on generic factors they are guessing will work because of what's worked for others in the past.

Practice: Design the right nudges

Once you've gained an understanding of the obstacles between occupants and their desired behaviors, start digging into the research on how people are influenced by their surroundings. For decades, psychologists, biologists, medical researchers, and public health officials have been studying these environmental effects in places like schools, hospitals, offices, and public spaces. Use their insights to improve how you think about the nudges you'll create.

You can also ask prompting questions to discover how the design should influence people. For instance, prompt your clients (or family members) to finish these sentences:

I want the space to transform people by . . .
I want people to experience . . .
I want people to interact so that . . .
I want people to feel . . .

An example of a strong nudge in action: As of this writing, when people think of a "technologist" or "computer scientist," they likely think of a white or Asian man. Research suggests that this is due to an overrepresentation of white and Asian men in those fields and that underrepresented minorities, especially young students, don't see people in tech who look like them.[10] This is why representation matters. Seeing a greater diversity of people—Black, brown, white, female, male, young, old, etc.—participating in computer science is likely to push your mind to reconsider who is capable of it.

So when a major tech company asked me to design a campus where Black and Hispanic students would spend a year studying engineering alongside professional tech workers, I recognized it as an opportunity to use nudges to change how people thought and felt, specifically about who "belonged" in tech.

My big realization was that if you're a twenty-year-old Black or brown kid on that company's campus, you're probably terrified. Hardly anyone looks like you. What I did was plaster billboards of successful Black and Hispanic engineers all around the campus. Now, as the kids walk around campus, they see billboards of successful engineers of color. They can feel like someone else has been in their shoes and made it happen, like it's possible. I placed the billboards so that company hiring managers could see them as well. If they see the success stories of Black and brown folks, maybe they will start to shed biases and see the potential in these kids. Nudges have the power to change how we behave and also how we think and feel—about ourselves and about those who may be different from us.

Practice: Create a strong push

As a rule of thumb, one nudge usually won't cut it. You need several nudges to make a difference.

If we're designing a hospital room, for example, we want patients to feel calm, relaxed, and replenished to support their recovery. A mistake would be thinking that just one design element will sufficiently create that experience—for instance, hanging framed artwork of nature or plants—when really, we should be thinking about the acoustics, lighting, comfort of the bed, and temperature of the room as well. Consider also where they might place personal items, notes of healing and encouragement, or drawings from loved ones. Many aspects of the space beyond what patients and visitors see on the walls determine whether people feel calm and replenished.

As you're designing, resist the temptation to make any one nudge do all the heavy lifting to create the intended impact. Instead, think about the ways you can use multiple aspects of design to get there.

Nudges are small but mighty. They hold tremendous power to shape our behavior without requiring us to do any thinking, and they can make the desired action the default. But what happens when our circumstances change and the space needs to grow or evolve in a different direction? That brings us to part 2 of this chapter and the second meaning of *design for change*: designing for change over time.

CHANGE OVER TIME

It's often said that good architecture responds to functional needs. But what people need changes over time. How the space functioned thirty years ago may not be how it needs to function today, and it likely isn't how it will need to function thirty years from now. If you're focused on meeting only today's functional needs without considering how the building's form will help it adapt into the future, are you really designing with the right priorities in mind?

The second meaning of *design for change* refers to this need to ensure that buildings can grow with the people using the space. As the designer, you need a form that can adapt and be useful as functions change. You also need to design for certain functions that are more timeless and enduring, not ones that may be fleeting.

Changes happen at different speeds and scales depending on who you're designing for. Homes, schools, hospitals, and workplaces all experience occupant turnover at different rates. Their cultures, ways of living, and functioning change along different timescales.

While it may make sense when designing your home to take only your family's opinions into account, designing a public building strictly based on one person's or group's opinion may neglect what's best for most people. It also creates a risk of making the design obsolete when those decision-makers leave. Once they are no longer the "owners" of the place, the remaining occupants will be left to cope with a space that could be ill-suited to their needs.

When I design schools, for example, I don't tailor classrooms around a particular subject or curriculum because what schools teach changes over time. Instead, I design a school's spaces based on timeless ways of learning: listening, observing, doing, making, debating, presenting, and discussing. As the school's curriculum evolves, I've ensured that their building still satisfies their needs because it's designed around the enduring functions of school, not the fleeting education fads of the day.

The same logic applies to a home. If you're designing a room within your home or designing the entire home itself, think about how you might want to live in the future, not just now. Are you planning to start or grow a family? Could an aging relative come to live with you? None of us knows what the future holds, so use that uncertainty to your advantage. Try to envision how modifiable the place could be for changes in lifestyle—for example, losing mobility and needing to get around with a walker or wheelchair. (I learned this firsthand after my mom suffered spinal cord damage and we discovered that her home, with its narrow hallways and sharp turns, was not built to support someone in a wheelchair.)

Designing so that the building can change over time is rare. Many designers work to create the "perfect" design for a singular outcome and then walk away to pursue their next project, never to return. But no building is static. Its occupants and their needs are always changing as people use the space for some time and then move on to occupy other spaces. Life is constantly in flux.

Office spaces, for example, undergo countless changes as leaders cycle in and out, bringing new management theories, ways of working, and desires for how physical space should enable work. One estimate says that changes in communication technology are so cyclical that buildings need to be rewired every seven years on average.[11] How can we expect any company to thrive in an environment that was designed for a completely different era many years ago?

Inevitably, societies change; priorities change; technologies change. When we *design for change*, not only are we looking to nudge people toward better lives, but we're designing so their buildings can change with them.

HOW TO DESIGN FOR CHANGE OVER TIME

You don't have to be an oracle to successfully design for change over time. In many cases, it involves resisting the common impulses we feel when going into a new project: focusing too heavily on the present at the expense of the future, wrapping the space too tightly around today's technology, catering to the whims of one individual or group of people whose departure may undermine the design's usefulness, and designing something people perceive as a fragile work of art and are too afraid to use. Keeping these priorities in mind will help you focus more on the future and on what designs could work no matter how that future takes shape.

Practice: Design around universal needs

In commercial and institutional buildings, the occupants change frequently, so this strategy is best for such projects. When people describe their wishes for the space, interpret what they say more generally. Try to synthesize their desires into a set of points universally applicable to a lot of people. This way, you can avoid getting bogged down in idiosyncrasies that could make your design obsolete when those people leave.

In addition, it helps to recognize that personal preferences show up in ways that are separate from the design itself. For instance, in office buildings, people express themselves through the photographs, mementos, and other objects they use to decorate their workspaces. Since people frequently come and go, resist the temptation to capture these idiosyncrasies broadly, such as in the building's space plan, services, or structure.

Mindshift: Adopt the long view

We shouldn't be building with the expectation that the structure will probably get knocked down in thirty years. Such a mindset leads to a self-fulfilling prophecy: We build quickly, cheaply, and without considering the people who may use the space in the future, so the final product doesn't allow for adaptive reuse, leading to enormous amounts of waste that we assumed was inevitable but wasn't. Instead, build with the intention that this structure will last forever.

We must ask ourselves better questions that treat designs as long-lasting. How can we accommodate the changing needs and functions in the coming decades? How might the function of the space change? How will the materials wear? How will the individuals using the space change? By asking these questions, you will be in a better mindset to design than if you had charged ahead assuming the building had an expiration date.

To help you attain the right mindset, try imagining how the building will change over time. If you're a designer, you can even render how the building will look not just today but fifty years from now. Force yourself to mentally inhabit this future world. This is hard work, and you may think it's difficult enough designing for the present, let alone some unknowable future. But it's worth striving for because it allows the design to continue to grow and evolve.

Practice: Conduct scenario planning

When we design a building, we're predicting how people will use it now and in the future. For this reason, the best buildings have a certain quality of forgiveness. The more tightly buildings are designed around the needs of today, the less adaptable they are to future conditions. We need places that can adapt to our evolving needs, not confine us to a plan set in place years ago.

Through scenario planning, we can wisely design places that are ready to evolve. Unlike most design methods that help us converge on a single, optimal solution that meets the needs of today, scenario planning is about divergence and preparing for many possible futures.[12] You can conduct scenario planning with your family if you're designing a home or with any group of people you're designing for.

As an example, let's say you're planning a new school building. The first step is to identify why you're building. In this case, your goal may be to add better spaces on campus for art, music, and self-expression. Once you're clear on what you want to achieve, make a list of the driving forces that can affect your future and the space's future. For the school looking

The more tightly buildings are designed around the needs of today, the less adaptable they are to future conditions.

to elevate the student experience, you may end up with a dozen or so forces: changes in educational technology, increase or decrease in funding or the operational budget, teacher shortages, development activity nearby, an increase or decrease in student population, changes in the curriculum and class offerings, and perhaps more public transportation added by the city.

Now rank the forces into two categories: important versus uncertain. You can do this by asking, Which of these driving forces are most important and would have a large impact on the building? Which are more uncertain and unpredictable?

Next you'll want to write out what you hope happens in the future if everything goes as planned. This is the official scenario. But because the future is difficult to predict, we can't count on that scenario coming to fruition. So let's plan for other scenarios.

Review your list of the most important and most uncertain driving forces. Imagine a scenario where a couple of these changes occurred. For the school, one possibility is that their student population shrinks but they maintain the same curriculum offerings. Another possible future is a growing student population and changes to the curriculum. In this way, select three or four alternate realities that could happen in the future.

With these alternate realities in front of you, it's time to strategize what will allow you to meet the needs of today without causing too much friction if one of these alternate realities comes true. How can the school create facilities for art, music, and self-expression while accommodating the future possibility of having a smaller school with fewer students or finding that they need to further expand their campus and change their classrooms for new subjects and curricula?

If the school has fewer students, it might want to sell off or lease one of its buildings. To leave room for that, the new spaces could be separate from the existing buildings on campus so it's easier to off-load a portion of the property. If the curriculum changes and classrooms need to be reconfigured, the interior walls could be built as stud walls with columns instead of concrete masonry block so that walls are not load-bearing and can be moved freely. Conversely, to allow for the possibility that the school needs to expand to accommodate more students, the new building could have a sturdier structure, allowing for the addition of another floor if it ever became necessary. These are design strategies that scenario planning can help you generate. If you entertain possible future conditions, you'll think about how to prepare for them.

Practice: Design for independence between layers of architecture

For a building to be adaptive, there must be separation—or "slippage"—between the various architectural layers. Either the people using the space or their designer must be able to make changes to one set of layers without undoing or destroying the surrounding layers. There are five layers to keep in mind: the structure (the frame of the building), the skin (the exterior of the building), the services (the mechanical, electrical, plumbing, and other utilities), the space plan (the layout of interior wall partitions), and the stuff (the furnishings).[13] Without slippage between these layers, it becomes invasive and costly to make repairs or upgrades. To update one layer, you must tear up or adjust several others in the process.

For example, say you design the building so it has a grid of columns holding it up. That's your structure. And then you have interior partitions to create the rooms. That's your space plan. In this case, your structure and space plan have slippage because the two can be freely modified without disturbing the other. However, let's say you make your interior partitions load bearing. Now the space plan becomes *part of* the structure, which means if you want to change the size or shape of the rooms, you have to disturb the structure. Without slippage in this case, you can't just change the space plan; you have to change the structure too.

When you design for layered independence at the start, you can more easily make changes over time that preserve other layers as they were originally constructed. Adapting the building when layers can be adjusted independently is more affordable, less time-consuming, and less labor-intensive.

Practice: Invest in a "loose fit" to allow for future adaptations

There's a reason people praise sturdy old buildings as having "good bones." A building's structure is one of the most important things you can invest in when designing a space.

Well-built structures allow for decades or centuries of ongoing modifications, such as retrofitting new electrical services or building additional stories. Foundations and structure should be capable of many lives: renovation, adaptive reuse, and retrofit. That's obviously well beyond the lifetimes of any of the people using the space, but construction for a long life allows buildings to be modified more easily and affordably over the long term. Plus, it's more sustainable than tearing down a building and rebuilding from scratch.

In addition to investing in a solid structure, consider the value of creating a "loose fit" in the size of the building and the services you install when starting out. That means getting more space than you presently need and overdoing the infrastructure up front—installing overcapacity electrical feeders and breakers, oversize chases, and an excess of outlets—so that the building is more adaptable in the long run. (This is most relevant for commercial and institutional buildings.) Spending too much on finishes at the expense of these services may make the design "sexier" from a visual perspective, but your occupants will be far happier in ten or twenty years when they don't have to spend exorbitant sums of money to rewire the building or install an extra electrical breaker because they've outgrown the initial design.

Practice: Make it comfortable for occupants to invest in changes

When designers think more in terms of what makes a space visually striking, they tend to make a space as lavish as the project's budget will allow. In the hopes of maximizing the design, any bit of surplus money quickly gets funneled into another splashy feature that will make people happier in the short term but won't necessarily enhance their long-term well-being or performance.

What this approach forgets is that upgrades cost money. Wouldn't it be a smarter strategy to invest in certain aspects of the building but then leave some money set aside for when changes need to happen?

For instance, I often encourage the people I'm designing for to invest in things like the structure so that the building has good bones, even if it means spending less on finishes. That way they have money left in their pockets if they find that the design needs to adapt to a new set of needs. You get a similar effect when you make a building energy efficient. Not only is this better for humans and all life in the long run, but it saves money that the building owners can put toward modifications later so their space stays current with their needs.

I also encourage people to take a "lite" approach to the technology they integrate into their spaces given how quickly it can become outdated. There's no inherent harm (and often great benefit) to enabling a space with certain capabilities. But tying the technology too tightly to the space—for instance, embedding hardware directly into the infrastructure of the walls—makes it expensive and difficult to remove. It also violates the best practice we saw earlier around preserving independence between architectural layers.

If the tech is so tightly woven into the fabric of the design that removing or updating it creates a great expense or hassle, it's not worth the trouble. Better to find a more ad hoc solution that can be installed and replaced as needed.

Lastly, it's good practice before walls and ceilings close—when all the wires, conduits, ducts, and bracings are exposed and visible—to photograph every wall and ceiling and tag it on the plans. This becomes a visual record of what's in the walls so people feel more comfortable changing things. If you're designing for yourself, save this information as a User's Manual that you keep someplace safe. If you're designing for someone else, give it to them at the end of the project so they can reference it later. Knowledge is power.

Practice: Revisit the design

Once you finish a project, even if you've taken all the previous steps into account, you still can't assume that it will be perfect for the rest of time. If we're serious about *design for change*, we must actively seek to learn how the design is or isn't adapting to suit people's needs. Isn't this how we ensure that our buildings remain just as well used and beloved as the first day we unveiled them?

Some designers don't *design for change* because they don't stick around to *see* change. They don't go back to see how conditions have shifted and evolved and how people are using the space differently. By forcing yourself to be aware that things change and going back to collect data on how well the design has held up, instead of choosing to stay ignorant, you become a better designer in the process. The exercise will also reveal just how much changes over time. The next time you're designing, you will keep this in mind and not try to fix things too rigidly.

The people you're designing for might not pay your research much mind. Because they intrinsically feel good or bad in the space, they don't need data to know how they feel. But it's important to treat the research you collect as an investment in you becoming a better designer. Our world needs better designers.

Practice: Teach people how to modify and improve their spaces
Spaces are meant to be lived in and used. They aren't public art pieces whose only job is to be admired. Nor are they supposed to be masterpieces that can't be touched, modified, or adapted, lest the people using the space ruin the designer's "perfect" creation.

In fact, the occupants control the space. It's theirs. It was designed for them, and they should have agency in modifying the space how they see fit.

Once projects are complete, I like to give people a tour of their new space and show them how things work. So much goes into a given design; only a fraction of it may be obvious at first glance. That's why I like to offer the space's owners suggestions for modifications they could make, showing that they won't break the space if they make changes and how the designs are meant to serve their needs. These efforts matter because unless people feel comfortable calling a new space their own, they'll never make full use of its ability to change over time.

PUTTING IDEAS INTO PRACTICE

In Baltimore, Maryland, *design for change* is what allows City Neighbors High School to become more than just a building that houses students—rather, the school's design changes the relationships between students and teachers, which influences how kids learn.

For example, most schools don't have spaces for kids to break away and enjoy some independence. City Neighbors installed alcoves outside the classrooms, which are visible through a set of windows so the teacher inside the room can still see their students. The alcoves have benches with seats that are wider than usual, allowing multiple kids to meet up and work. This simple design has changed the way classes are run: Teachers are nudged to let their students break away for periods of time, while students remain nearby in case they need to rejoin the group.

In the cafeteria, another great design feature has changed relationships between students and teachers. On the walls are framed photographs of teachers when they were young children. There's even a photo of the school principal when he was a young boy at the kitchen table with his big brother. This has humanized the teachers for the students. It has made it easier to connect with them since they can see that faculty members were once like them—they, too, used to love video games or playing pranks with their siblings. Thoughtful design features like these make richer connections possible.

When we *design for change*, on the one hand we're recognizing design's power to influence us. Sometimes that happens quietly, almost imperceptibly, based on the way a space is laid out and nudges us in certain directions. It's also our job as designers to uncover visions of the future with the people we're designing for. The future must feel as palpable as the present. Future needs must feel as pressing as the ones staring at us from current agendas and to-do lists. We will miss our targets at times. Your plans will occasionally fall apart. The future is impossible to predict. But by designing based on the scenarios most likely to take place, without backing yourself into a corner with any single decision, you can create spaces that properly serve people for years to come.

As historian and philosopher John Ruskin implored, "When we build, let us think that we build forever. Let it not be for present delight, nor for present use alone; let it be such work as our descendants will thank us for."[14]

To start designing for change, ask yourself: *How do I want to nudge people through this design? What will allow the space to adapt over time?*

8

FOLLOW NATURE

We need to create designs that recognize human beings' place in the order of things.

PRESERVE AN ANCIENT CONNECTION

It was the most important test of my life, and I nearly bombed it.

It was 2002. I was seventeen, a senior in high school, and I was taking the standardized test that awaited nearly every high school senior with ambitions of going to college: the SAT. That Saturday morning, I was sitting in a packed classroom with two dozen other nervous teenagers, and all of us were grappling with the same set of frustrations. No, not the word problems in the math section or the tests of vocabulary in the verbal section. We were all fighting against something much worse: the roars of construction from the bathroom next door.

The constant loud rumbling from drilling, hammering, and materials crashing to the floor was a nightmare. I was already so preoccupied with the exam itself, including fear of running out of time, that having to deal with the clanging and banging of construction made everything much worse. *Who the hell decided to schedule construction on the same day as the SATs?* Focusing was impossible. At no point during the three-hour exam did I feel confident about my test-taking abilities. When I walked out, I was sure it had been a complete waste of time.

In fact, I felt so unconfident about my scores that I immediately signed up to retake the test a month later. Thankfully, the room was dead quiet that day. I could pour all my attention and energy into acing the problems I'd studied so hard to master. And you know what? My scores proved it. My score on the second test was 130 points higher than the test I took in the noisy room. I didn't do any extra studying between the two tests. I didn't change my test-taking strategy. Everything stayed the same except the space where I took the exam.

I'm sure you've had a similar experience at some point. When we're in a space that meets our biological needs, we know it. Rooms with plenty of light, fresh air, a comfortable temperature, and a range of sight lines that allow our eyes to move between focus and relaxation just make us feel good. More alert. More present. Since we feel our best, we're able to perform our best.

As a student of Baaham, remember that our environments influence us in subtle but powerful ways. This challenges our conventional understanding of who or what is at fault when things don't go the way we planned. Typically, we blame ourselves or other people. If students underperform, we often blame them and tell them to try harder, rather than questioning their learning environments. The same is true for measuring employees' performance at work. How often do we look at people's working environments when trying to understand why the quality of their work has slipped? How often do we simply assume they've gotten sloppy or lazy?

Baaham encourages us to look beyond perceived character flaws. It acknowledges that our physical spaces can be designed in ways that support our physiological needs, professional duties, and personal goals and desires.

The problem is, when we look for solutions, our search usually doesn't go far enough. We design solutions with the assumption that we, as humans, know best without considering whether other species may have developed their own solutions that we could borrow and learn from. In the vast time line of the universe, we basically didn't arrive until last Tuesday. Millions of species of plants, animals, and insects have been adapting and surviving for much longer than we've been around; we should learn from their designs. To ignore them is to endorse a form of human exceptionalism that usually leads to less effective design. Just as every

Millions of species of plants, animals, and insects have been adapting and surviving for much longer than we've been around; we should learn from their designs.

person you meet can teach you something you did not know, every species likely holds the same power when it comes to teaching us about design.

To *follow nature*, we must take our biological wiring into account when thinking about how a space should be designed. And when we do, we'd do well to draw inspiration from the organisms in nature that have devised their own time-tested solutions.

Take an example like America's suburbs. There, we find an environment marked by sharply manicured hedges and plant life shaped into perfect geometric boxes. We're trying to control nature. We use unnatural and harmful chemicals to kill certain species of plants for homogenous-looking lawns. These design choices make the environment feel artificial, weakening our connection to nature and risking harm to our health and well-being.

Meanwhile, when plants are left in a more natural state, you're more likely to notice them when you walk by. As you walk down a sidewalk lined with perfectly shaped hedges, you might not even notice them. But if they break the invisible plane between sidewalk and bush, naturally sticking out in places, you're more likely to touch them, think about their existence, and be affected by them.

We must take our biological wiring into account when thinking about how a space should be designed.

We also have an opportunity to take inspiration from nature in the way we gather and incorporate feedback about our designs so we can better adapt and survive. For instance, peppered moths have wings that look remarkably like tree bark, which they use to defend against certain species of birds. Over time, the moths with lighter wings weren't as camouflaged as those with darker wings, so they got eaten more. The ones with darker wings avoided becoming prey, so darker wings became the dominant trait. Similarly, when we have a design that works well—and better than others—that should become the dominant (adopted) design.

When we build, we can collect the same kind of feedback about how previous attempts went. In nature—and in design and construction—delayed feedback causes solutions that aren't working to be repeated, rather than eliminated. But if our antennae stay tuned to improving upon the current design, each new project becomes more supportive and life-giving than the last. One of the factors that complicates this process is when unhelpful designs proliferate, similar to glitchy genetic mutations in nature.

As we saw in chapter 3, social media plays a major role in this rapid proliferation of trendy designs. When we cater to online algorithms, rather than focusing on what works and iterating on those solutions, we tend to produce designs that are far more radical than useful. Such designs don't make use of what worked in the past, nor do they focus on making natural and gradual improvements like nature does. We end up concocting some bold aberration that doesn't benefit from all the time-tested and feedback-responsive adaptations that came before it. For example, picture a public plaza designed without shops, restaurants, and seating to bring it to life. Instead, it's surrounded by buildings without public amenities on the ground floor, so the plaza feels cold and unwelcoming. Or imagine a building with such acute angles that you feel compressed inside the building and have a hard time using the narrow spaces, so those areas go to waste.

Follow nature compels us to head in the opposite direction—to embrace the ways our biology responds to our environment and to design so that we harness the wisdom of the evolutionary process. When we *follow nature*, we're able to create spaces that put us in harmony with our surroundings. We stop fighting our environment and, instead, allow it to support us.

HOW TO FOLLOW NATURE

In one sense, *follow nature* means gaining an understanding of how nature evolves certain practices over time and then discerning which practices help us create more effective designs. In another sense, it means creating design conditions that support our biology as humans, such as the right amounts of sunlight, airflow, openness, stimulation, and the presence of natural forms. Adopting best practices ensures that your design works with, not against, the built-in relationships to nature we all share.

Practice: Design with humans' biological needs and limits in mind

Our own evolution has hardwired certain sensitivities into our biology, which we should look to incorporate—or avoid—in our design process. These include but aren't limited to light, stimulation, air, noise, openness, movement, and an affinity for nature.

Light

The circadian system, through light-dark patterns reaching the back of our eyes, tells us when to go to sleep and when to wake up. We can use this sensitivity in how we design in a handful of ways.

For example, a body of research shows that exposure to daylight first thing in the morning signals to the photoreceptors in the back of our eyes that it's time wake up and start activity.[1] The brain's "master clock," located in the suprachiasmatic nucleus, receives these light signals and regulates our physiology and metabolism throughout the day.[2] One way to incorporate this design into your home is to build the bedroom separate from the rest of the house so that, upon waking, you have to cross through a sunroom or onto an outdoor patio, where you can stretch, sip coffee, and soak in the morning light for a few minutes.

If those photoreceptors aren't triggered because we didn't get adequate light, our master clock will be off. This is why, from a design perspective, we risk harming our health, productivity, and thinking if the spaces where we spend most our time, like homes, offices, and schools, are not well lit. When the Georgia Institute of Technology and Emory University did studies of the homes of seniors, they found that the seniors whose homes had less natural light—due to, say, smaller windows—got less light exposure overall, had more disrupted sleep patterns, had greater rates of insomnia, and showed higher rates of depression. Separate research even links circadian disruption and increased risk of cancer.[3]

Another way to design using humans' sensitivity to light is by following the sun's path over the course of the day. In the northern hemisphere, the sun's arc passes along the south side of a building, which means an office on that side will have full sun exposure, more glare on screens, and be hotter throughout the day. Meanwhile, an office with windows facing north will get a bright, even glow without changing sun patterns or glare, but it will generally be colder because this side is in the shade and doesn't get direct sun.

If you like warmth and can handle the heat or if you have a shady tree outside, consider sitting next to a south-facing window. If you prefer a less dynamic light condition, where the sun isn't in motion, and are okay in colder spaces, the north side will be good for your desk. You'll get nice, even lighting all day long.

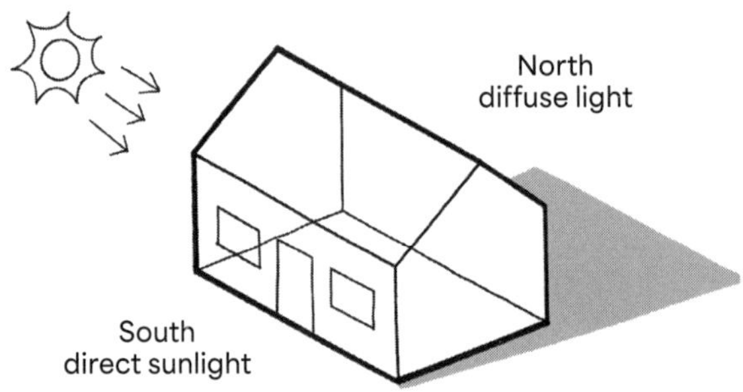

Stimulation

The amount of stimulation in an environment affects people's mood and ability to focus. However, many modern spaces are devoid of the kind of complexity that is found in nature and that our minds require for optimal well-being. Instead of living and working in environments with soothing natural tones, visually interesting features, and the softness found in nature, a substantial percentage of the population labors within labyrinth-like buildings with stark interiors that provide little sensory stimuli. Nothing could be further disassociated from our need for stimulation.

When we're immersed in a natural environment, we experience a phenomenon known as "biophilic engagement." Our bodies relax while our minds remain alert, activating what biologists call an automatic relaxation response.[6] It's the opposite of the body's fight, flight, freeze, or fawn response. You may have experienced this during a recent hike or nature walk, as your nervous system seemed to calm down. This is the opposite of how people live in uber dense cities: crowded spaces contained by glass and cement, where nature is largely absent but stress and fatigue are rampant, causing productivity to plummet. To alleviate these symptoms, we must find ways to access nature to elicit biophilic engagement within our confined artificial environments.

But we need to be careful about the stimuli to which we expose people: Too much stimuli, or the wrong kind, can be detrimental. For example, I like to take walks to think. But if it's too windy or too cold and I'm not dressed appropriately, I won't be able to focus. I'll be too preoccupied with the weather. When something is distracting you, too much of your cognitive processing power gets diverted to the wrong task. Instead, we should strive to expose people to natural stimuli and give them complexity—like the kind found in nature—without overwhelming them.

Air

The quality of our air has real but underappreciated effects on our overall health and performance within a space. For example, research has shown that well-ventilated office spaces improve employees' cognitive function compared to spaces that allow a buildup of carbon dioxide, which can lead to negative effects like headaches, fatigue, restlessness, and trouble thinking or concentrating.[4] One study found that in an office where carbon dioxide rose from 550 to 1,400 parts per million (ppm), people's cognitive ability scores dropped by 50 percent.[5] Outside fresh air, for reference, has a typical carbon dioxide level of 400 ppm.

Other research has shown that cleaner air affects whether students show up to school. Currently, asthma is a leading cause of absenteeism, responsible for more than twenty million missed school days in the U.S. per year.[6] One study showed that after installing an electromagnetic air cleaner in classrooms, absenteeism dropped from 8.3 percent to 3.7 percent. After the air purifier was removed, the rate jumped back up to 7.9 percent.[7]

One of the more ingenious designs I've come across for promoting airflow was from the Harvard Center for Green Buildings and Cities. The team at Harvard built an office with window sensors that would sense when the carbon dioxide levels were too high and would trigger the windows to open automatically, circulating fresh air. Solutions like this are especially helpful because they are a good reminder of how to realign with our biological needs when largely invisible factors, like poor air quality, threaten our well-being.

Noise

Consider this: A study of more than one thousand second-graders in twenty-nine German schools found that aircraft noise exposure at home was associated with small but significant increases in headaches and stomachaches.[8] Separate research found that poor acoustics in classrooms causes students to perform up to 20 percent worse on tests.[9] But it's not just students who suffer from excess noise. From the 1960s to the early 2000s, noise levels in hospitals more than doubled.[10] And they've continued to increase, leading to an increase in patient stress.[11] Similarly, patients who are heard (or even seen) between curtains are less likely to speak openly with their doctors, which can result in misdiagnosis, according to one study.[12]

These findings tell a story about noise that we as designers should take seriously and apply broadly. Similar to overstimulation, excess noise overwhelms and sometimes obliterates our ability to focus. When designing, consider how to turn down the volume in spaces where people need peace and quiet to live and work well. One solution at home is to build closets between rooms to mitigate noise transfer, so for instance, one person moving about won't disturb another person who's sleeping.

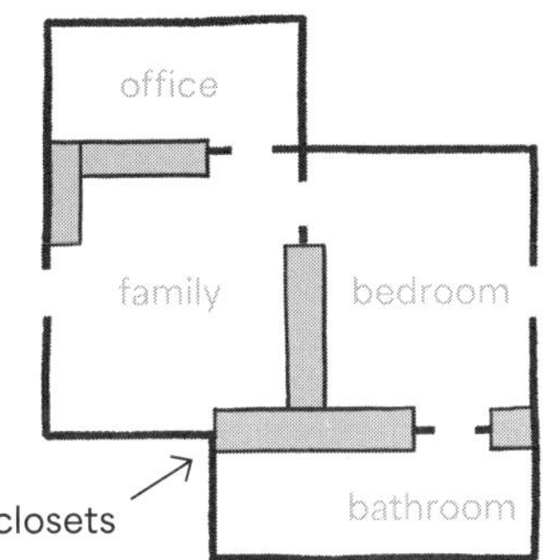

Openness

According to environmental psychologists, our sense of openness influences how quickly or slowly we perceive time.[13] In tight spaces, time seems to pass more quickly. But in wide-open spaces, time seems to pass more slowly. Imagine sitting on the beach and staring into a vast space that hardly changes. Time seems to stand still. This is different from how we feel sitting in a home office under a low ceiling, staring at a wall. Our mind and time feel like they're racing.

When this happens, our breathing also changes. When we go outside and stare at something in the distance, like a tall tree hundreds of feet away, it changes how we breathe—we're able to take deeper breaths, like a weight's been lifted from our chests. The expansiveness of the space does that.

Consider how this might impact your working environment. In a smaller space, like a cramped office with barely enough space to move, a looming deadline might fill you with anxiety. But if you were working in a spacious room with soaring ceilings and vast open space, you might feel calmer about the work. Look to design with our sensitivity to openness in mind. How might you use this insight to create a more effective environment for yourself and others?

Movement

Our ancient ancestors scaled craggy rocks, foraged through dense forests, and walked many miles to survive. Many remote tribes still track down food on foot. This should tell us that our bodies are meant to move and that our spaces should facilitate that movement. Unfortunately, many contemporary designs have prioritized convenience over all else, removing the need for strenuous movement.

But this isn't the case everywhere. In many parts of Southeast Asia, families don't use dining tables, opting instead to eat sitting on the floor. Not only does the practice serve as a nudge toward healthier behaviors that promote mobility later in life, but the bending and squatting required to sit and stand puts people in better alignment with how their joints and muscles were designed to move in the first place. Smarter design understands how our bodies age and what we need to stay healthy.

Affinity for Nature

Our biophilia means we have a preference for nature itself. In other words, it's not just that we respond well to natural light, open spaces, and fresh air. Researchers believe we have an underlying desire to connect with the natural world, making us want to be closer to forests, rivers, mountains, grasslands, parks, and the outdoors in general. The biophilia hypothesis may explain the large body of research showing how even short exposures to nature tend to increase people's sense of well-being, reduce stress, and improve overall health.[14]

Biophilic design, then, incorporates this hypothesis into the enclosure, positioning, and features of a space. It strengthens relationships between the people using the space and the natural world around them. Perhaps the most common way we do this is through houseplants, which are both pleasurable to look at and may even lead to enhanced cognitive function.[15] In school settings, psychologists have found that students who have a view of nature perform better on tests of concentration than students who view another building or who don't have windows at all.[16] Other studies have shown that the effect may be even greater: One pilot study found that sixth-graders who spent the entire school year in a biophilic classroom with a garden view, natural lighting, and nature-inspired patterns on the walls and floor saw their test scores increase by more than three times the gains of the students in ordinary classrooms.[17] The researchers also saw a 7.2 percent increase in the number of students testing at grade level among kids in the biophilic classroom. Clearly, incorporating elements of nature into our designs can have profound effects on how people think and feel in those spaces.

Practice: Learn from how other species design.

Compared to other species, humans have been around for only a short while. To put it into perspective, if you measured the history of the Earth as the length of your arm from shoulder to fingertip, the entirety of human history would live on the tip of your fingernail.

What this means is that humans have had far less time for trial and error than most other organisms. Given that things in nature generally improve over time, those organisms have had far more time to adapt and evolve and devise solutions to their problems. Shouldn't we look to these more experienced organisms for inspiration on how to design?

Biomimicry is a field of design rooted in that concept. When we look at plants, we can observe how they turn sunlight into fuel and use that information to refine how we harness solar power for energy. When we look at wasps, we can learn from the additive construction process—adding one thin layer at a time—they use to build their nests so we can advance the way we 3-D print our own products and structures. And when we look at termites, we can see how they build their mounds with heat escape hatches to stay cool in hot climates; we can use such "passive" cooling strategies to regulate temperatures in people's homes without using as much energy.

Observing these practices can also challenge assumptions we may have about how we build. For example, when wasps build additively, there is no waste. But the way we build creates a lot of waste. Sticks of lumber come in certain lengths and sheets of wood in certain sizes, and when we position those side by side to create the length we want, we often chop off the excess, which gets discarded as waste. Or when we pour concrete, wooden formwork is built (essentially a cast) to hold the wet concrete. That formwork becomes waste material after the concrete dries.

If we used additive methods like a wasp, we wouldn't create that waste. This is what 3-D printing allows—it lets us escape conforming to right angles. Currently, we use so many right angles in design because that's how our materials arrive to us. They are straight, flat, and rectangular—essentially a kit of parts built upon straight and perpendicular lines. Mimicking the way a wasp builds lets us surround ourselves with new kinds of forms and shapes, which can create different spatial experiences and relationships and open a new formal language: We can create environments that weren't possible before and that change how we experience the world. These sustainable designs create no waste and work with the natural environment—much like plants, insects, and other organisms have for millions of years.

Practice: Collect feedback

Feedback loops are everywhere in nature, and because of these feedback loops, nature has evolved over billions of years to become more accomplished. Designs have improved. For any species, its shape and features have evolved in response to feedback from the outside world as to what has been working and aiding the species' survival. Several species of katydid insects, for example, have evolved over hundreds of millions of years so they can perfectly mimic surrounding plant life, including with leaflike wings and sticklike bodies, so they stay hidden from predators. These adaptations formed gradually to help the organism survive.

We have the opportunity to evolve too. Every building is an experiment we can learn from. Over the years, our architecture has become more complex—new buildings are bejeweled with fancy mechanical systems, audiovisual features, security measures, and responsive building controls—but they haven't necessarily become more accomplished. That's because we don't collect feedback. Doing so would allow us to learn what's working and what's not so that future buildings can be better made.

For example, I used to live in a quaint neighborhood where the landlord built several new structures. Rainwater gutters were installed on each of these small buildings, but the ends of the gutters pointed toward the walking paths, directing water where people would walk. I pointed out to the landlord that the gutters were making the paths slippery, which could lead to someone falling and getting injured. They also were directing rainwater over hard surfaces, and this runoff could lead to flooding—not to mention wasted water in a drought-prone state like California. All of these issues are known; humans have experienced these tribulations before. So why are we repeating the mistake?

Simply rotating the gutter ends by ninety degrees would have diverted the water into plants and ground surrounding the structures, which would have nourished the plants and soil, kept the sidewalks from getting slippery, and avoided water waste. The landlord, unfortunately, didn't see these opportunities as worth his time. No changes were made.

In cases like these, since we don't collect feedback like other organisms in nature, we repeat the mistakes of the past and allow bad designs to persist unchallenged for decades and sometimes centuries. When we don't use accumulated knowledge, we repeat mistakes, needlessly making life worse for ourselves and, in certain cases, hurting our species' chance at survival.

A great way to collect feedback on your design is to conduct post-occupancy evaluations. Ideally, you would complete four rounds of evaluation. First, one month before people start using the space, ask about their expectations. Use that as a baseline. Then, return six months later to see how the space is living up to those expectations. Return a couple years later to check in on the space. See how it continues to serve people and how conditions may have changed in unexpected ways. Finally, consider going back at the ten-year mark to see how the building has adapted with the passage of time.

This sequence of evaluations lets you see any initial pleasant surprises or problems occupants face, which adjustments they made, and how well the space has adapted to people's changing needs over time.

We must remember that feedback teaches organisms what adaptations to make in order to live better. And feedback shows us what adaptations we should make to architecture so it serves us better. Improving on what we've done is the only way our designs can lock in more of what works and omit what doesn't serve us. That's what every organism has done for millions of years and what humans ought to do every time one project ends and the next one comes into focus.

Practice: Mimic both form and function

True biomimicry involves borrowing the form and function of a plant or animal species, and it should happen on both the macro and micro level.

Let's say you're designing a building, and you're inspired by the trees in your area. Ask yourself: *What would make the building treelike?* Don't stop at mimicking the form of the tree. Go deeper to borrow the functionality of the tree, mimicking how it converts light and water into energy, how it filters the air, and how it uses shade to maintain comfortable temperatures.

A real-life example of a treelike building is the Bullitt Center in Seattle, Washington. This six-story office building collects, filters, and disinfects water using its rainwater collection system. Like the soil around a tree, the building was designed with composters that turn human waste generated on-site into fertilizer using two rows of five aerobic composters.

The building's windows feature shades that rotate based on the exact location of the sun, just like a tree. And like a tree's leafy canopy, the rooftop features an array of 575 solar panels that extend beyond the building's edge to produce approximately 230,000 kilowatt-hours of electricity per year.[18] That's enough energy to power twenty-one single-family homes for one year.

Furnish your space with details that reflect nature's benefits. For instance, a painting of a bright-blue sky won't set your circadian rhythm like a balcony or terrace that lets you step outside to experience the real thing. The painting might be nice to look at, but it won't satisfy your biological needs. Opt for the real-life version of whatever natural elements you wish to incorporate into your design.

Mindshift: Prioritize light, air, and open views

Sometimes designers will create spaces that physically restrict the people who use a space from accessing the natural elements that matter most—things like sunlight, fresh air, and open views. Missing any of these elements reduces the quality of our experiences in some way. We should design our spaces such that people remain in connection with the natural elements.

For instance, imagine being in a sunny, well-ventilated space that was no bigger than a prison cell. Your experience would feel limiting, and your eyes would strain from having only short focal lengths to focus your vision. Likewise, if you were in a space that was expansive and had fresh air but relied only on artificial lighting, it might feel depressing, and you might experience headaches. And finally, if the space felt wide open with great sunlight, but the air was stale and filled with carbon dioxide, you'd soon feel tired and unwell.

On the other hand, think about how pleasant spaces are when they have both long and short sight lines to let your eyes focus at different lengths, when they have natural light to set your circadian rhythm and make you more comfortable, and when they let in outside air that refreshes and rejuvenates your body. If you're not in a space where this is possible, use your awareness of the principle and remember to get outside frequently for fresh air, natural light, and distant views—because your body needs all three.

PUTTING IDEAS INTO PRACTICE

One of my favorite spaces that exemplifies *follow nature* is the Connected Classroom I designed for a school in rural Alabama. Students attending this school needed more help than most: Fewer than 2 percent of students in this town were proficient in math, and just 5 percent were proficient in science. I knew the classroom had to provide a better learning environment, in part by supporting kids' biological needs.

The design of the Connected Classroom follows nature in several ways. Special technology was installed in overhead light fixtures to mimic the energizing effects of sunlight and to keep students alert. Carpet flooring, a high-performance acoustic ceiling, and recycled polyester wall fabric all help to mitigate noise so students can easily hear their instructor and each other and not get distracted when doing focused work. Laptop stands were 3-D printed from the wood of a fallen ash tree. And blue and green hues were chosen because they've been shown to promote feelings of calm and creativity, helping combat the frenzy of a school day.

A number of other features, specifically designed to enhance students' focus, include a "pace track" pattern on the carpet. This is a predefined loop around the room demarcated by a different color on the carpet to provide a clear walking aisle for students to move around and to promote active thinking. There are also perforated wooden screens around the study booths, providing a sense of privacy and distraction-free separation from others while still filtering in soft natural light. To help students focus on what's being displayed on the large screen at the front of the room, the screen is surrounded by a darkened stage area, providing a frame that makes it easier to focus on the content (the same way many phones and laptops today feature a dark edge that helps you focus on the content in the center). All of this happens in a room with minimal visual stimuli (because we know cluttered walls distract students) and nontoxic paints, which keep the air microbe-free for students.

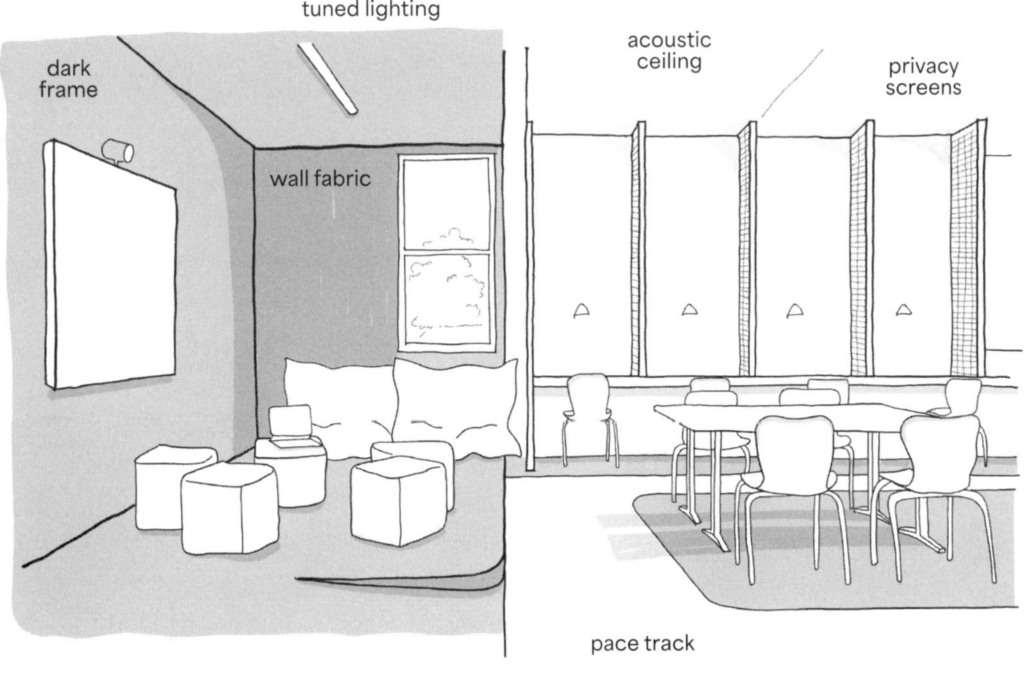

+ + +

When we *follow nature*, we begin to incorporate all the elements that tap into our ancient human preferences and processes. We are not separate from the world. We are a part of it. Missing this crucial element is to miss a vital aspect of Baaham's core insight: that we influence our environments and they influence us—on biological, physiological, and emotional levels. The natural forces around and within us are unavoidable. The choice we must make is how to harness them for our benefit.

To start following nature, ask yourself: *What biological needs should this space meet for people?*

9

EMBRACE DETAILS

We need to recognize the power of small things to make a big difference.

TWO SETS OF DETAILS

Everything you've learned to do so far—*look within, solve important problems, design for change, follow nature*—should give you a clear idea, or vision, of what your design should be and do. But how well the space realizes that vision and helps you achieve your goals hinges on how much you focus on the finer points.

That brings us to our next Baaham principle: *embrace details*. Because even something as small as whether you use a nail or screw can mean the difference between safety and devastation.

Here's what I mean: If you talk to hurricane survivors in the American Southeast, they'll tell you how important it is that their metal roofs are fastened with screws rather than nails. This is because screws hold down roofs better than nails, which get pulled out by the heavy winds. The difference may be small, but the impact is life-altering.[1]

Embrace details captures two kinds of details, both of which are crucial for creating a design that works and puts us at ease: functional details and visual details. Together, these make a difference on a practical level because the space is easier and more effective to use, on a personal level because the details meet people's objectives for the space, on an emotional level because the details create greater feelings of comfort for everyone using the space, and on an ecological level because the design minimizes harm to the planet.

Functional details are about making the space work well for its purpose. If we ignore the functional details, we risk creating a space that's inconvenient to use, full of little frictions that make life harder. When the functional details aren't right, it can feel like your environment is constantly fighting you, working against you, putting obstacles between you and what you want. On the other hand, when we pay attention to functional details, we're able to create spaces that are enjoyable and easy. You can almost feel the care that was put into creating that space, as if the designer knew you'd be coming and wanted to make sure the space catered to *you*.

I've encountered both situations many times in my life. I'm sure you have too. Let me share a few examples.

When we pay attention to functional details, we're able to create spaces that are enjoyable and easy.

Near my home, there's a grocery store that does something strange with its berries. Rather than keep the berries in bins that are chilled, like how most other stores tend to keep them, this store simply puts the berries in bins at room temperature. From a distance, you might not notice that this has any impact on the berries. But up close, it's clear the berries are mushier and more shriveled than those at other grocery stores, and some are actually rotting. In this case, the functional detail of the berries' container has a major impact on how well the design works—that is, whether the berries I buy taste good and how much I enjoy eating them. If the store had embraced details in the design for the berry display, I'm sure it would have saved money by reducing wasted berries and making customers happier.

Fortunately, I've also had the pleasure of being in places where great functional details made the experience much more enjoyable.

On vacation a few years ago, my partner and I stayed with some friends in their home for about a week. They had recently bought the home from previous owners, who had it custom-built rather than buying a spec home from a developer. In their construction, the prior owners clearly paid attention to functional details in many thoughtful ways. I kept finding them over the course of our stay.

For instance, the kitchen had a separate faucet for piping hot water, which made it easier to make tea in the morning. In the bathrooms, the holder for toilet paper was designed so you could easily replace rolls by rotating the holder rather than popping in a spring-loaded tube. In the bedroom closets, the drawers had soft closes that slowly closed the drawer without banging. And when I sat down to work, the desk had lighting conveniently installed on the underside of the upper cabinets, which illuminated the work surface more evenly than an overhead ceiling light, which would have cast a shadow from my body being in the way.

Such examples are meant to illustrate how functional details in built designs can affect everyday experiences. But even the transportation infrastructure we use to move between spaces has details that matter.

When I was traveling in France some years ago, I noticed that the maps on the Paris Métro were inconveniently located on the train car walls right above where people were sitting. If I wanted to review the full map of the Métro, I had to stand directly in front of the strangers sitting down and bend awkwardly close to them to read the map. This didn't make me (or the strangers whose personal space I violated) feel very good. The placement of the map was a poor design detail. Its function was to make people feel more comfortable and oriented, but it created an uncomfortable interaction in the process.

Alternatively, the Métro stations themselves tended to get the functional details right. As I left the train and made my way to the exit, I often came across two maps on the wall: one at the city scale, meant to orient me within Paris, and one at the block level so I could see what streets were nearby. This predates smartphones with GPS, so as a traveler in a foreign country, those maps made the experience of navigating an unfamiliar area much easier. And it was because of their designs—specifically, their helpful placement in the station and their different scales—that the maps performed their intended function.

Across all these examples of functional details, design has the ability to inspire powerful emotions. It deeply affects how we feel, like when you walk into an old cathedral and find yourself in awe at the soaring ceilings and intricate stonework. The magnitude and atmosphere of the cathedral make you slow down, soften your voice, and feel more contemplative. You may feel a sense of peace. The building is creating this for you.

In this way, part of a space's function (and usually one of its goals) is to make people feel a certain way. You can achieve this by having details that create the right mood or, as I call them, the right "emotional ergonomics." Just like an office chair or sofa can be physically ergonomic and contour to the natural shape of your body, spaces that are emotionally ergonomic contour to the feelings people want to have in a particular space.

Spas that allow you to forget every earthly concern are emotionally ergonomic. Meanwhile, the cheap spa in New York City that I would go to when I didn't have much money—the one where I could hear every car horn outside and every footstep on the creaky wood floors and where dozens of distracting laminated signs about state laws and payment options were on the wall—was not emotionally ergonomic. The massages were fine, but I was never able to fully slip into a feeling of relaxation. This is why it's important to think holistically about the environment you're creating. Its details can alter people's emotions and experience.

The details that make a space's emotional ergonomics include aesthetics, lighting, sound, and textures. And depending on how much you pay attention to each of these details in your design, you can dramatically improve or throw off a space's emotional ergonomics. Creating the right mood is difficult when the details don't work.

We see the power of small details in many aspects of life, even beyond architecture. One study of chocolate bars, for example, found that people tended to rate the chocolate as sweeter when the sharp corners had been rounded off and made smooth.[2] If the edges of a chocolate bar can change how it tastes, imagine how the thousands of tiny details in a space affect how we feel.

The other set of details are visual details. They are what make a place feel beautiful and put people at ease, and humans universally appreciate certain compositions because of our affinity for and evolution in nature.

Making buildings visually appealing—and not merely functional—matters because humans are visual creatures. When we're awake, our vision accounts for two-thirds of all electrical activity in the brain, or approximately two billion of the three billion neurons that are firing every second.[3] But it's not just any visual stimulation that we tend to prefer. Regardless of a person's preferred style or taste, everyone carries an encoded preference for certain visual compositions. How well you incorporate these aesthetic principles into your design will determine whether people enjoy being in a space or feel an itch to go someplace else.

One of the core insights about our visual preferences is that we tend to prefer complexity and repetition.[4] We evolved in natural environments like plains and deserts and jungles, where we saw complexity and repetition in plant structures, animal coats, mineral formations, and landscapes. Think of a pinecone's layered spiral structure or a leopard's spots. These kinds of repetitive and slightly asymmetrical forms, which occur in the natural world, continue to be most compelling in our architecture. We should be mindful to include them in our designs.

What we often get, though, is monotony. Many buildings are built with little to no regard for our hardwired aesthetic preferences, deferring instead to minimalist details that aren't offensive but also aren't inspiring or exciting. Mostly, they're plain and boring.

Real estate developers may believe that this means their buildings are safe and uncontroversial, but the more palpable effect is a sense of dreariness, devoid of spirit. A plaster wall with subtle imperfections and mineral-based paint, which lets you see imperfections, is far more satisfying for most people than a gypsum wall that's perfectly flat with a solid paint that makes it look like a manufactured panel. Mass production has stripped imperfections from our environments, but nature has imperfections.

These imperfections create subtle variations that break monotonous repetition. We need variation. We need complexity. This is partly why people tend to find old European towns and cathedrals so charming. Those places don't feel at all mass-produced. They were built with a strong eye toward and an appreciation for details.

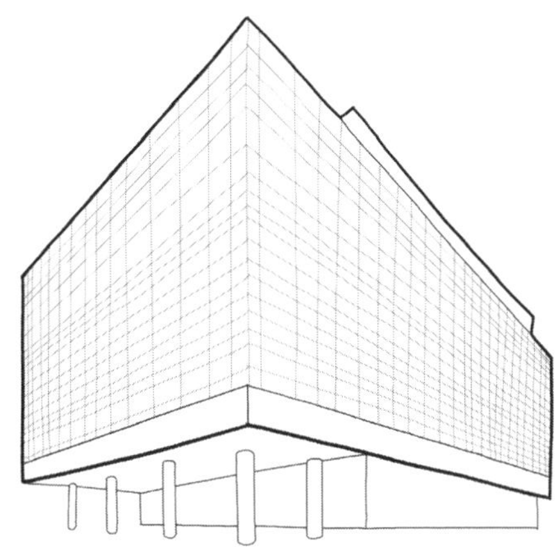

monotonous designs are everywhere

We have the power to make beautiful buildings, and we should, because life can be mundane day-to-day. When buildings are bleak and bereft of beauty, they contribute to feelings of dreariness. When we make our environments beautiful, they can be uplifting. They make our experiences better. And often, when spaces are exquisitely crafted with extraordinary details, they make us marvel at human capability. They inspire us to create marvelous things ourselves because we're endowed with a feeling of possibility and because we've just witnessed our potential.

When buildings have thoughtful details that make them easier to use and more beautiful, they also last longer. We're less likely to tear them down. For the future health of our planet, this matters a great deal. In the U.S. alone, roughly one billion square feet of buildings are knocked down each year, and the average lifespan of a building is just forty years.[5]

When spaces are exquisitely crafted with extraordinary details, they make us marvel at human capability.

Details make buildings more sustainable because people feel attached to the building's beauty and character, so they work harder to maintain it, making regular repairs and keeping it in good working order for decades or centuries to come.

HOW TO EMBRACE DETAILS

Embrace details means thinking about the subtle and nuanced facets of design that guide how well a space works for its purpose and how people feel about it. Here are ways you can incorporate this principle into your projects.

Functional Details

Practice: Track and satisfy the project's criteria

Here's an exercise I like for figuring out which details to include in a design project.

First, list all the important criteria that must be met, including every objective to achieve and every problem to solve. Think of each as a lightbulb that's turned on. Until you satisfy that criterion, the bulb stays on, indicating something you need to address. As a designer, your goal is to create solutions that turn the lightbulbs off.[6] You should come up with a way to track your criteria and which bulbs are turned on or off, whether it's handwritten notes, a spreadsheet, or another system that works for you. What you'll quickly find—and this is what makes the exercise so tricky—is that satisfying some of the criteria negates others.

Let's say you have two criteria: lots of natural light and energy efficiency. You satisfy the need for energy efficiency by having exterior walls made of straw-insulated panels. You "turn off the light" for that criterion. To bring in lots of natural light, you add windows in the facade. This lets you "turn off the light" for the natural light criterion. But by introducing so much glass, you allow heat to escape the home in the winter and enter the home in the summer, which means the lightbulb for energy efficiency turns back on.

To make progress on your design, your goal is to satisfy all criteria. If any lightbulbs turn back on, keep designing until they can be turned off again. Along the way, try not to let outside constraints influence your ability to turn off all the bulbs. For example, if a manager says we can't continue designing until we turn most lightbulbs off because that will cost more, I would say maybe things *should* cost more before we bring them into the world, because they'll have long-term impact.

We should spend time designing until we get the right solutions. This process helps us remember the important criteria all the way through a project, regardless of how many people are influencing the design.

Mindshift: Calibrate the emotional ergonomics

Have you ever sat in the waiting room at a doctor's office with nonstop reality TV or national news blaring in the background? Perhaps the intent is to distract people from the stress of their upcoming appointments, but I find that the combination of noise and on-screen drama just makes for a more anxious experience.

A far better alternative would be to play soft, soothing ambient music like the kind you find at a spa. Patients would feel more at ease, have more presence of mind to think about what they want to discuss during their appointment, and perhaps feel comforted enough to share openly with their doctor, which could improve their treatment.[7]

Emotional ergonomics is a concept that can help you identify which details will help evoke the emotions you're after.

In every project, I use dozens of design elements to create the right emotional experience. There are the more obvious elements, such as wall color and furniture. But the list also includes some nonobvious elements, including but not limited to sounds, technology, lighting (not just a light fixture's aesthetics but also its lumens, color, temperature, and positioning), graphics, textures and materials, views, and volume. In their own way, all of these design elements contribute to an environment's emotional ergonomics: whether the space feels calming, energizing, contemplative, or social.

Spaces inform our emotions. By considering the emotional ergonomics you're creating, you can make sure that emotion is the desired one.

Practice: Make in-life decisions

Whether we're designing for ourselves or others, we have a responsibility to include the details that will make the design work better.

It can be hard to remember this when we're shopping for fixtures, furniture, paint, and materials. We are visual creatures, after all, so it's no surprise that we're drawn to the way the various elements look together. But the way to *embrace details* at this stage is to adopt a mindset I call making "in-life decisions." It's the opposite of making "in-store decisions," which is how most people tend to buy things.

An in-store decision is when you're looking at a sink faucet online or at a shop, get attracted to how it looks, and decide to use that for your project. If you were making an in-life decision, you would consider not only how the faucet looks but also whether the faucet spout is deep enough to reach the center of the sink so people have enough space to maneuver their hands without hitting the back. And you would consider what type of handle makes the most sense based on how you want to control the water for the activities you'll be doing at this sink.

Making in-life decisions is about thinking practically about how things will be used and by whom. When choosing a product or material, ask: *What is the primary function I need this item to perform, and how well does it do it?* So if you buy a mailbox, test opening and closing it. Is it sharp, and do you risk getting cut every time you put your hand inside? Or can you pull out mail and packages easily?

It's easy to get swept up in the thrill of finding a coveted decoration or building material that you believe will enhance the design. But when you're selecting a product or material, be sure to think about its practicality. Otherwise, you'll end up with design features that may look good at first glance but don't function well—something you'll be forced to live with every day.

Visual Details

Practice: Compose natural forms

Generally speaking, humans aren't drawn to random compositions or monotonous ones. Randomness can feel alarming or threatening, and monotonous repetition can feel boring and dreary. When buildings look unstructured (random) or symmetrical without interruption or variation (monotonous), people tend to react negatively. Think of a building whose windows are either randomly scattered or repeated in a relentless grid. Neither arrangement is likely to feel pleasing.

Nature simply doesn't have geometrical configurations with monotonous or simplistic repetition. Even if you look at the hexagonal cells of a honeycomb, each cell has minor imperfections. On a tree, every leaf is different. Slight imperfections, or variations, are why nature doesn't feel industrial. So how can we mimic nature and create environments that feel more natural and appealing? I recommend drawing from several tactics.[8]

Add variety

Interrupt a perfect symmetry to create more variety like we see in nature by introducing small differences (similar to the slight imperfections of honeycomb hexagons) in the repeating elements. For example, if you look at most modern buildings, the columns of a building are typically uniform. They look mass-produced and identical to one another. You could introduce variety by adding different details on each column. So, from a distance, the columns are still approximately the same, just like leaves on a tree, but as you get closer, you notice their variety. If you had a row of repeating columns, this would be enough to shift it from monotonous to interesting.

This is also why some brick walls look better than others. When a wall is made of bricks that all look identical—they are the same color, have the same texture and shape, and clearly look manufactured or mass-produced—it never feels quite as good as the brick walls where each brick has its own character: some slightly darker than others, a handful of them with some moss growth, not all installed perfectly in plane, and some with mortar scraped across the front. Each one is perfectly imperfect.

Cluster repeating elements

Say you have a wall in your bedroom with closet doors, six of them in a row, each touching one another like the modernist storage walls you see on social media. There's no hierarchy—nothing stands out—in a design like that. It's a monotonous repetition of door after door after door. A simple way to break the monotony is to form a cluster with the repeating element (a single door, in this case) by framing three doors together so that you have two groups of three doors. You could do this by adding a continuous frame around the outside of the three doors or even by engraving a frame on the doors themselves that's inset from the edge and runs across the length of three doors, visually binding them into a group. This type of clustering can be used to break the monotony of repeating elements and introduce some complexity through hierarchy.

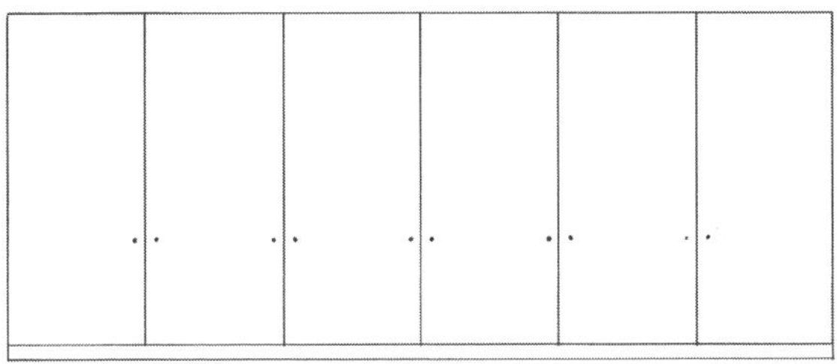

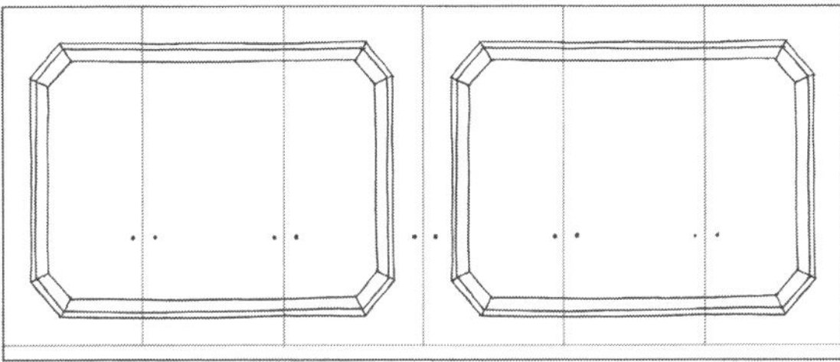

Insert an intermediary scale

As humans, we're used to being surrounded by fractals because they're everywhere in nature—in trees, clouds, rivers, plants, fruits, snowflakes, and even our own respiratory and vascular systems. Essentially, a fractal is when a shape (or physical form) is made up of smaller shapes that resemble the larger form, and those smaller shapes are made up of even smaller shapes that resemble them. Trees are fractals because the trunk shoots out into branches that look like mini versions of the main trunk, and from those branches shoot twigs that look like mini branches. It's a structure consisting of self-similar forms repeating at different scales, and we're accustomed to this pattern. Architecture also feels more natural when it contains varying scales, and grouping elements into a fractal form helps us introduce new scales.

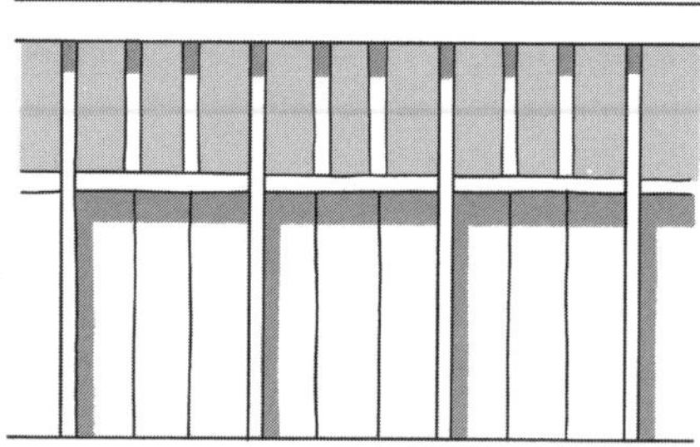

To illustrate, imagine facing a blank wall. That's one scale, the size of the entire wall. To make it feel better, we could add an intermediary scale in the form of a fractal. Divide the length of the wall into three sections. The large wall now has three parts that we're going to clearly define by framing each part. This is a new scale we've introduced that's smaller than the scale of the full wall. Let's do it again: Split each of the three framed areas into thirds. Then infill each of those thirds with slats. Now we've got a wall with four or five scales instead of two. By adding intermediary scales, we have a form that's more similar to nature, less boring, and more pleasant.

Alternate the repeating elements

When a single element repeats over and over—AAAAAA—there's no rhythm. If we add a second element and alternate the two—ABABAB—it creates a pleasing rhythm. This is true in music, art, and architecture. A lot of buildings feel monotonous and boring because they lack rhythm. Have you ever seen a facade with the same window repeating itself like AAAAAA? An easy way to create rhythm and interest would be to add details to the windows so that there are two types. We don't even have to change their shape and size—all we need are some finer details so it's clear there's a type-A and type-B window. Then alternate those types to create an ABABAB pattern.

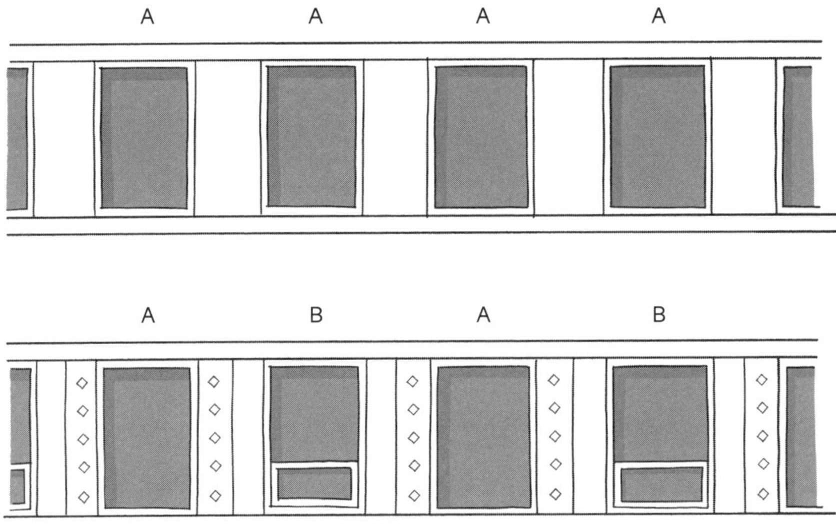

This is a simplistic rhythm and can help break up the boringness of AAAAAA. But if we repeat AB too many times, even that will get boring. If our facade has thirty windows, this simple rhythm won't be enough, and we'll want to insert an intermediary scale or cluster the windows into groups to create some structured hierarchy for better rhythm.

Create a gradient

Gradient effects—identical repeated elements that gradually decrease in size or intensity as they repeat—are another way of making more natural forms. Gradients occur in nature and were often used in preindustrial structures, such as Chinese pagodas with their tiered and telescoping roof structures. You can create a gradient effect across a single wall, around a building, or even across a line of buildings. In each case, it will make the environment more calming because you'll be breaking its artificial monotony.

Mindshift: Make it special

Think of the buildings you love. They probably weren't mass-produced or built just to make money; more likely they are singular creations that have real intention behind them with a certain kind of charm thoughtfully included in the design.

You can introduce these elements into your design with ornamentation that makes the building or space feel unlike any other, even if the flourishes are subtle. By replacing flat or blank walls with such details, the space will feel more special to you and be more eye-catching and pleasing to others. This feeling of care is important because it turns an ordinary design into something worth preserving for generations.

PUTTING IDEAS INTO PRACTICE

One of the greatest examples of *embrace details* is the Salle Labrouste reading room at the Bibliothèque Nationale de France, the national library of France. I was nineteen the first time I stepped inside. When I came back twenty years later, more accustomed to the kinds of structures we typically build, I was in awe. I found myself inspecting and appreciating every detail, my eyes slowly tracking up and down each column, across each railing, around each lamp and table, taking in all the care that had been put into making this place.

Built by French architect Henri Labrouste in the 1860s, the reading room's signature details include nine majestic domes held up by slender iron columns adorned with metal reliefs in the shapes of plants and natural forms. Even the structural framing that supports the underside of the arches is unlike typical solid framing. It was created like a lattice structure, so instead of a bulky beam, it feels like a delicate piece of custom metalwork with the rhythm of raised rivets and infill panels that look like compasses or solar flares. These let light pass through from the glass oculi down to readers, making the structure feel light and airy.

Along the side of the reading room is a wall of books, but that's not all it is. Above the books are three recessed arches with engraved blocks adorning the entire underside of each arch. Inside the arched shapes are murals that depict the natural world with blue skies and green foliage.

The details on the shelving and flooring are equally stunning. Near the stacks of books along the edge of the room are shorter shelves whose tops aren't flat but are slanted at the right angle for you to open a book and comfortably browse through its contents. This reduces strain on your neck, versus a flat surface, where you'd have to lean over the book and tilt your head down. Even the air vents on the herringbone-patterned wood floor are custom-made with geometric tessellations. Sitting or standing in the space, everything feels cared for, which makes the library as a whole feel functional and special.

As we saw in *Design for Change*, the mindset of the designer should be to create something that will stand for many generations. In that instance, we were talking about the value of using sturdy materials and building methods and allowing for adaptation over time. Here, having a mind toward longevity matters because it influences how careful you are in considering the details of the design. In the short term, staying detail-oriented will offer people a number of functional, psychological, and emotional benefits.

In the long term, these details serve a protective function: They make a space worth caring about. They give the people using the space good reasons to maintain it and preserve the beauty they see in it. While this has obvious personal benefits to the space's occupants, it also upholds the

Baaham ethos of designing in a way that protects our natural resources and the planet as a whole. Such is the mighty power of details.

To start embracing details, ask yourself: *What finer points must I not lose sight of while designing? How can I make this space beautiful?*

10

BUILD ECOLOGICALLY

We can design sustainably—and make places feel unique—by using local materials and solutions.

CONSIDER YOUR ECOSYSTEM

As of this writing, humanity faces critical challenges around the depletion of resources, the degradation of ecosystems, and climate instability. The way we build is part of the problem. Approximately 11 percent of the annual global carbon emissions that contribute to the rapidly changing climate come from construction and building materials. That's five times more than the carbon emissions from the entire aviation industry.[1]

All of us play a part in this, particularly professional designers, engineers, manufacturers, and developers. As I write this, I am working with a middle school in Atlanta—one that happens to be located on the exact block where I grew up—to develop a multiuse building on their campus where kids can learn robotics and science, practice subjects like art and music, and have a gym to run around and play.

The campus sits on a three-acre property and has one four-story building, which has a parking lot in the front and backs up to an undeveloped wooded lot. Before the school's administrators hired me, their thought was to put the new building where the current parking lot is and pave the wooded lot to build a new parking lot. This didn't make sense to me. They already had a parking lot, so why go to the trouble of ripping it up—wasting money and raw materials—just to move it someplace else? Instead, we decided the parking lot will stay put, and the new building will go in the wooded lot.

This is more ecologically friendly for several reasons.

First, we're designing the building around the location of the existing trees so we can preserve as many as possible. But keeping the building close to the trees also means the school will be shaded in the hot sun, which lets students enjoy cooler temperatures and has less of an impact on the school's energy usage. Not to mention, the trees will filter the air and absorb excess rainwater, lowering the chances that a big rainstorm could cause flooding from the runoff.

Even if we need to cut down some trees in the process, we're working with a contractor to use the felled lumber to build some of the facade of the building, along with window and doorframes and even some of the furniture. We're also reusing old materials from past projects, thanks to a seventy-thousand-square-foot warehouse in town operated by the non-profit Lifecycle Building Center, which salvages building components such as floor and ceiling tiles, carpets, and fixtures. It then sells those reclaimed pieces back to customers at a discount. We're making generous use of this service throughout the school's construction as a way to give new life to old materials.

Together, these practices will help make the building's carbon footprint as small as possible. Instead of making costly, unsustainable changes to the landscape, our team of arborists, landscape architects, civil engineers, and energy and sustainability consultants are finding creative ways to shrink the impact of the building over its lifetime.

Build ecologically means thinking about how our actions—planning, designing, constructing, operating, developing, and redeveloping—affect the ecosystem we're part of and optimizing our actions to minimize harm and prioritize regeneration. It means not ordering the chair that must be shipped halfway around the world just because it looks slightly better. It means not rushing the process to save money. It means not treating natural landscapes as ours for the taking, for human use only.

Building ecologically means prioritizing smart design over sexy design. Responsibility over profit. Modesty over excess.

Doing the right thing can be hard. A lot of money is involved. A designer who doesn't research healthy and sustainable materials, who doesn't shape the design by conducting an analysis of how the building will use energy

Building ecologically means prioritizing smart design over sexy design. Responsibility over profit. Modesty over excess.

during operation, and who doesn't think of ways to minimize disruption to nature and local ecosystems will certainly save time and, thus, make more money on their project. And a developer who doesn't require a designer to do all of this will pay less for design services, finish faster, and get tenants in sooner, collecting more months of rent.

When others don't share our sense of urgency to protect the planet, we struggle to bring about the changes we envision because the scale of this work is too ambitious to do alone. We must work with others to build society's spaces. Still, we can't let others' negativity deflate our spirit and lead us to abandon the cause altogether. Developing irresponsibly is potentially calamitous. A self-inflicted, avoidable, fatal blow. Baaham shows us how we can better serve ourselves and future generations.

HOW TO BUILD ECOLOGICALLY

Since many of our climate-related challenges stem from a globalizing world, Baaham focuses on designing in ways that shorten the distance between your project site and the people and resources that can bring the project to life. Whether you're a design professional or a design lover who's renovating your home, we all share this responsibility.

Building ecologically also involves being a good steward of the planet in other ways, such as using materials that can be reused multiple times with minimal risk of toxicity, staying sensitive to nearby habitats, and treating other species' lives as equal in value to our own. Our needs, and the needs of the planet, must be able to coexist within our designs.

Practice: Source local materials and products

As a rule, closer is better. Materials sourced from nearby usually require less energy to be transported to your project site than materials obtained from farther away. Look for brickyards, quarries, and wood mills that are in or around the town of the project. They'll most likely be producing bricks, lumber, and slabs and cladding using local clay, trees, and stone. Take a geographic approach in your search for materials rather than simply looking for the "ideal" materials regardless of where they're coming from.

Make sure "local" truly means local though. When I was designing that classroom for the school in rural Alabama, I was about to order a set of wall panels from a local manufacturer whose website said they were made in the U.S., but being skeptical, I gave them a call to learn more. It turned out the panels were made in China and only cut to size in the U.S., which meant the true environmental toll was many times greater than I first thought.

In addition to minimizing harm, sourcing materials locally has added benefits in that the natural elements used for your project—such as soil, trees, stone, sand—are already suited for that climate. The tree bark or straw thatch from the local plants has evolved in those geographic conditions and is likely to better withstand the local weather than bark or thatch imported from some other climate. Plus, since the materials are native and more familiar, there's a higher likelihood that local workers will have experience with them. When the building needs repairs as it ages, they're more likely to know how to take care of it. Use this mentality not just for materials, but also for products including the doors, windows, equipment, furniture, and so on. Search locally before you search afar.

Practice: Use renewable and healthy materials

When deciding which materials to use for your project, look for materials that are durable and nontoxic and that don't deplete finite resources.

In many regions, for example, wood is a better alternative to metal or brick, because it has a smaller carbon footprint (based on today's production methods) and is renewable, not finite. We can grow more wood, not more metal. We should try to use renewable materials such as wood, cork, or straw as often as possible and only turn to other materials when there are legitimate reasons.

To demonstrate how to choose between materials, let's compare different kinds of flooring. Luxury vinyl tile (LVT) is one option for you. But LVT is made from toxic plastic that releases harmful chemicals during

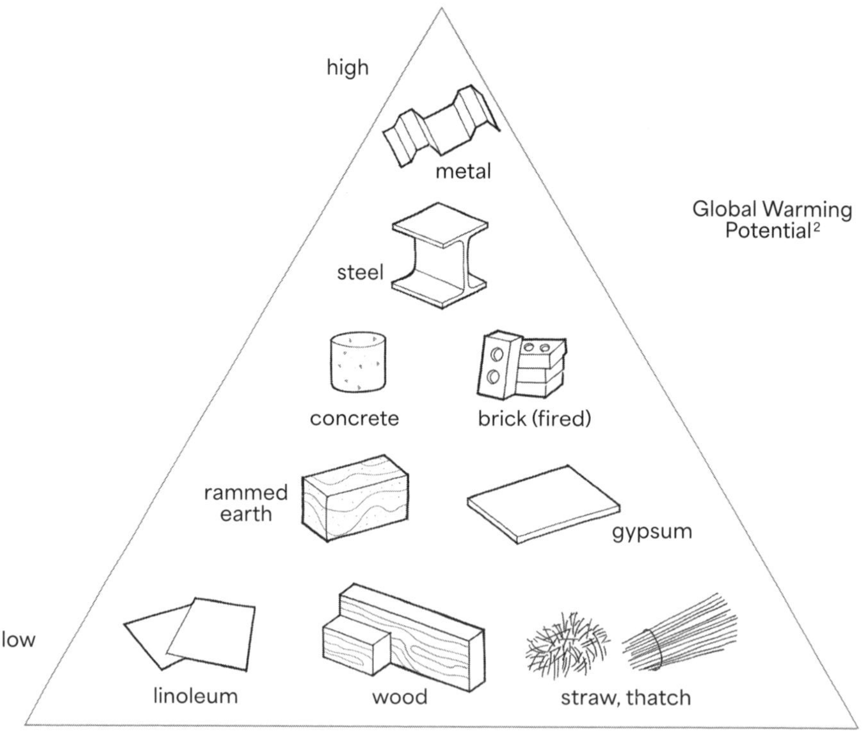

its production and disposal, which pollutes natural habitats and even the bodies of water we drink from. The manufacturing process is also energy-intensive, generating large amounts of greenhouse gas emissions.

Synthetic flooring materials like LVT are often promoted as better solutions than their natural counterparts, like traditional wood flooring, because they are more durable. But durability doesn't matter if new tenants move into an office and rip out the flooring because they don't like the style. In these cases, after only a few years of use, the LVT is tossed in a landfill, where it will take hundreds of years to decompose.

As an alternative, you could consider linoleum flooring. Instead of toxic plastic, it's made from natural materials like linseed oil, cork dust, and wood flour. The materials required to make linoleum are abundant natural resources that are renewable. The photosynthesis of the biobased materials used in linoleum provides carbon dioxide absorption that generally exceeds the carbon dioxide emissions caused by transportation and production. That means linoleum can be climate positive (or possibly carbon negative, meaning the linoleum removes more carbon from the atmosphere than its production generates) from the time raw materials are extracted until the final product ships from the factory. It's also durable and can last for decades, and when it's time to replace your flooring, the old linoleum is biodegradable or can be recycled into new linoleum.

Another alternative to LVT flooring is bamboo. Bamboo is a fast-growing grass, which makes it rapidly renewable and unlikely to get depleted. Growing it requires little water or fertilizer. While growing, the bamboo releases oxygen and absorbs carbon. And once it's made into flooring, it's durable and can last up to fifty years, so it doesn't need to be replaced frequently, which minimizes resource consumption over time.

As you search for eco-friendly materials, be wary of "greenwashing" practices by companies. Many companies use slick marketing and deceptive language to make you think a product is sustainable—for example, claiming it's "made from recycled materials"—when only 2 percent of its composition comes from reuse and even that portion is "pre-consumer," meaning the product never had a previous life because it was made from scraps at the factory and therefore isn't truly being recycled in the way we all understand the term. Look past the manufacturer's words; seek out numbers. This is where you'll find the truth about a product's sustainability.

Additionally, be wary of relying on local practices just because "that's how things are done around here." The most common method isn't necessarily the most sustainable; it might just be the easiest and cheapest approach. For example, most builders in the American Southeast build schools and community centers using concrete masonry unit (CMU) block walls. Are concrete blocks cheaper and easier to install than other materials? Generally yes, but with our current methods for producing concrete, there's a consequential carbon footprint. In those cases, I would say that if you have a more sustainable method in mind, do it. If you're the first or one of the first, you'll help the skilled workers in the area learn this new way of construction that's better for the environment. As workers become more skilled in the practice, the labor pool will grow, becoming more competitive and driving down costs.

Once you have achieved a good fit with your design—that is, you've followed the other Baaham principles and arrived at a working design—optimize for how much energy and material will be used for construction. This means making wise choices about which products and materials to use, considering whether they are renewable, how far they will travel, and what environmental toll their production will create. And if you happen to work for the government, consider this: How can you make it easier for people to buy products and materials that are better for the planet and, ultimately, better for society?

Practice: Design for aging

By choosing materials that are durable and age well, you'll reduce the future need for material consumption, harvesting, production, and transport. Materials like wood, brick, stone, and loam are not only durable, but they age attractively. Contrast them with other materials often used for building exteriors, like aluminum panels, which look worse as they age. When you use materials that don't age well, they likely will fall apart or get torn down because of how bad they look after a few years. That's not sustainable.

Another way to design for aging is by anticipating and accommodating future maintenance. If the building is easy to maintain, people will take care of it and extend its life. If it's difficult to maintain, it can fall into disrepair and get slated for demolition. For example, if your facade is made of large metal panels and a panel develops a crack over time, your options aren't great. Local experts may not have the specialized knowledge or skills to repair the manufactured panel. It may require having a manufacturer repair the panel or replace it entirely. Because of cost, the building's owner may hold off on repairs or replacement. Over time, the crack may worsen or allow water penetration and compromise other parts of the building.

Compare this to a building exterior that is made of many smaller elements like shingles, lapped board, or thatch. It's much easier for a building owner or local laborers to repair these smaller elements. This allows the building to be maintained over time. Unlike a metal panel, if a shingle cracks, it requires much less material, requires no cranes to install, and avoids transport of new material from far away.

Design architecture that's easy for people to care for, and they will.

Practice: Respond to climate and geography

Think about the geographic and climatic conditions of the place you're designing for. Is it rainy? Windy? Does it get extremely hot and dry? Be sure to design according to those conditions.

To do so, don't rely only on technology, because many technologies still run on harmful fossil fuels, making them ecologically unsound. Instead, seek out solutions that don't rely on exploiting finite resources. For instance, if your climate is extremely hot, turn to the passive heating and cooling strategies that have been employed for thousands of years in hot climates, such as in the Middle East. Even before the advent of air-conditioning, people living in extreme climates were able to maintain a comfortable temperature in their buildings with some clever design techniques. For example, they erected wind catchers (or wind towers) that rose above buildings to catch prevailing winds and direct them into the building, providing cross-ventilation and cooling.[3]

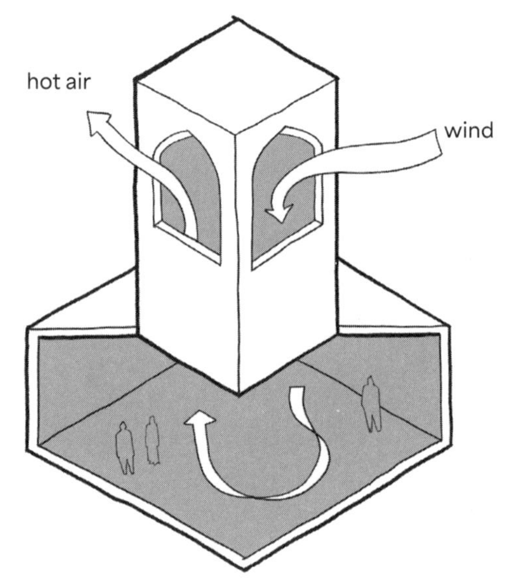

When you ignore how local communities have built for a long time, you risk making something that doesn't work for that context. In the hot and humid American South, for instance, homes were once built on stilts that lifted them a couple feet off the ground. This was to allow air circulation underneath the structure for natural cooling and to protect the homes against pests and water damage during heavy rains or floods. Over time, however, people began associating this design with lower-class living, so people abandoned the stilts and built their homes on the ground.

Suddenly, there was no air circulating under the home and the wood structure was in contact with the earth. The result: termites and wood rot.[4]

What got lost to time was that the raised home wasn't a style choice; it was a response to the local climate and served an important function. Rely on local knowledge. Look at how things have been done for generations and which solutions have endured for which reasons.

Practice: Reuse buildings

As a society, we need to think about how we live, how much space we take up, how many resources we use. One metric we can track is our utilization rate, or the amount of time a building is occupied. In general, our utilization rates are awful. A typical American school building is empty 82 percent of the year because it's rarely used in the evenings, over the weekends, or during the summer. Our offices are unused while we're at home, and our homes sit vacant while we're at work. Could there be more effective and efficient ways of living and working to make better use of our buildings? Building ecologically means thinking of smarter solutions so there's less waste and fewer underused or redundant structures. As you embark on your design, consider whether you need to build something from scratch or whether an existing structure can be renovated and retrofitted to meet your project's needs.

While new buildings are environmentally expensive, a renovation or an adaptive reuse—when a building designed for one purpose is put to different use—comes with a smaller ecological footprint. It requires less energy and fewer materials, and less waste is produced. Plus, rehabilitating an old building can help change the feeling of an entire neighborhood. It's an opportunity to take an unattractive block or area and make it attractive and useful for the community.

Even if a whole building can't be adapted to suit a new purpose, sometimes the rubble from old buildings can be reused. One technique for this is cyclopean masonry. In a process that's been around since ancient Greece, large boulders from the ruins of past structures are reused to make new walls. With thoughtful, calculated arrangement, the new walls are nearly solid without gaps despite using boulders of different shapes and sizes.[5]

We should consider how we can creatively use building waste for new construction, even if it feels difficult. We are better stewards for the planet when we take on the challenge of rehabilitating an older building and giving it a second or third life.

Mindshift: Be sensitive to habitats

Architecture is an act of care. It allows us to support human needs. But to truly care for humans, we can't think only of humans—we must care for the ecosystem we're part of. This includes the other species of plants and animals on Earth. Care for the ecosystem is care for ourselves, and disrupting our ecosystem rocks us in the process too.

The approach in the 1900s was about who could build the tallest buildings, the most monumental structures. Our competition moving forward should be "Which designers and developers can provide the most ecological care?" Initiate your project by asking how you can achieve the project's objectives while minimizing your ecological impact. What's the smallest footprint you can leave, both in terms of the actual footprint of the building (its size) as well as the unintended consequences you may generate by disrupting wildlife in the area?

One technique for preserving a place of beauty and flourishing ecosystems is to reverse the typical design mindset, which says to build on the most pristine plots of land and forsake the ugly, overgrown plots. Do the opposite. Build on the "undesirable" plots of land and beautify them in the process so that you can preserve what's already flourishing and enjoy them as beautiful scenery. By doing this, you raise the standard for the entire site, preserving what's worth preserving and giving new life to what needs repair.

PUTTING IDEAS INTO PRACTICE

To see *build ecologically* in practice, we can look to the David and Lucile Packard Foundation headquarters in Los Altos, California. With 915 rooftop solar panels, the building manages to offset 100 percent of its energy needs. To further conserve resources, rainwater is collected in a 20,000-gallon cistern, reducing the building's water usage by 40 percent.

In terms of sustainability, 95 percent of the building was made with recycled materials from preexisting buildings. The building itself is narrow, only forty feet at the widest point. This is so natural light can reach every square foot of the building's interior, reducing the need for artificial light sources. And 90 percent of the building's plants, arranged around and within the property, are native to California, eliminating the need for pesticides brought on by foreign plants.[6]

These features and more—including temperature-regulating windows, green spaces for wildlife, and permeable paving to reduce water runoff—add up to create a space that fully embraces an ecological approach to design.

Creating more Baaham spaces isn't enough to solve our climate crisis. But if the powers that be—our governments, real estate developers, planners, designers, and engineers—collectively decide to heed the call and build more ecologically, humans can make tremendous progress. And while none of us single-handedly caused environmental degradation, we all must live with the consequences, and that means sharing the responsibility in how we design.

Beyond preserving the health of the planet and our ecosystem, *build ecologically* has other benefits too. Research shows that people most enjoy places that have a strong sense of place and "could not be anywhere [else]."[7] People find joy in places that are scenic and that feel different from other places. That's why people flock to Venice for its canals, San Francisco for its hilly streets and streetcars, and Amsterdam for its narrow-gabled homes. Yet modern structures seem to be converging toward the same trendy aesthetic and losing all sense of place. Visit a chain coffee shop or corporate office anywhere in the world and it feels the same—regardless of whether you're in Honolulu or Houston, London or Lisbon, Tehran or Tokyo.

When we *build ecologically*—using local materials in ways that are responsive to climate and geography and reusing the buildings of our ancestors—we preserve and highlight a sense of place. Each town or city develops its own aesthetic. By responding to local conditions and using local resources, we help places develop and maintain a uniqueness that's worthy of experiencing.

When we don't design in a Baaham way and create spaces that aren't responsive to place, then everywhere starts to feel the same. When places feel the same, we don't feel like we're experiencing new things, travel becomes less fun, and ultimately, we experience less joy. Building ecologically isn't just prudent and necessary for survival; it's vital to happiness. And if we're not happy, it means we're not building the right kind of world.

To start building ecologically, ask yourself: *What local solutions already exist for my project type? How will I minimize environmental impact?*

11

ZOOM OUT

We need to see the bigger picture of how our designs fit within their surroundings.

NO DESIGN IS AN ISLAND

It's often said that "no man is an island" because we each depend on the people around us. We're all connected. The same is true with design. No window, wall, building, or city block is an island. At every scale, every design finds itself nestled within a larger context. Furniture and lighting fixtures are contained within a room. Walls are contained within a building. Buildings are contained within city blocks, which are themselves contained within the overall local environment. None of these pieces of the built environment operates in isolation. They all coexist in an ecosystem for living.

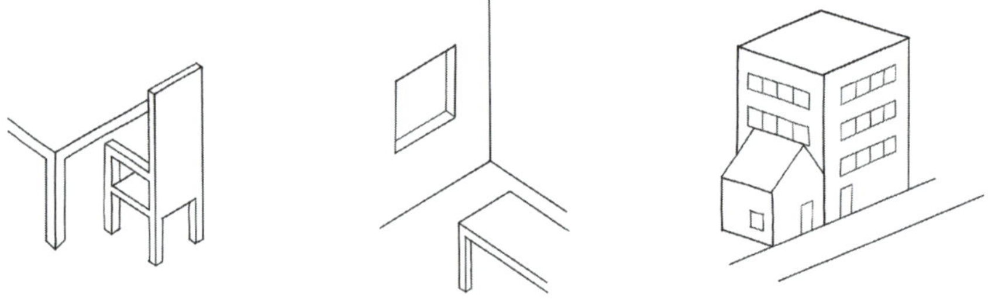

Everything has a larger context

Once you realize that every element in a design exists within a broader context, it will compel you to design differently—to focus on the *interactions* between design elements, not just how each works on its own. Just as it's the conductor's job to turn a group of musicians into an orchestra that produces a symphony, it's your job as the designer to turn individual elements of walls, floors, windows, doors, stairs, roofs, lights, furnishings, and landscape into a unified design that works well, serves its purpose, and makes people feel comfortable (or whatever feeling is desired depending on the space's goals).

Zoom out is the principle that lets you achieve this goal. It gives you more information about the context in which you're designing, because when we don't zoom out, we ignore all the invisible but real relationships that exist between objects and how the different parts interact with one another and with the people using the space.

What are the consequences of failing to *zoom out*? To begin with, you'll struggle with what to design.

For example, when I redesigned a middle school in Australia, I worked with the school to figure out what kind of educational experience they wanted for students, then zoomed out to look at what the neighborhood already offered so the school didn't repeat spaces that existed nearby. So rather than build a new performing arts center, we made use of the community's existing state-of-the-art performance center. And when I discovered that many of the students were skipping lunch because the school lacked an adequate cafeteria, I nudged the school to talk with the elementary school across the street about sharing their gym—which wasn't being fully utilized—so they could turn their own gym into a food hall. In addition, vendors from around town could set up stalls for the kids and community members to purchase food throughout the day and evening, as the school was located in a food desert.

By zooming out in the design process, the school and I were able to save its resources and money because they realized their community already offered certain things to students. We didn't need to build them from scratch.

A consequence of failing to *zoom out* is that your design won't effectively meet its objectives or solve your problems. Consider a small example: If you're choosing materials for a work desk, consider how the climate might affect the experience of using the desk. When I first moved to

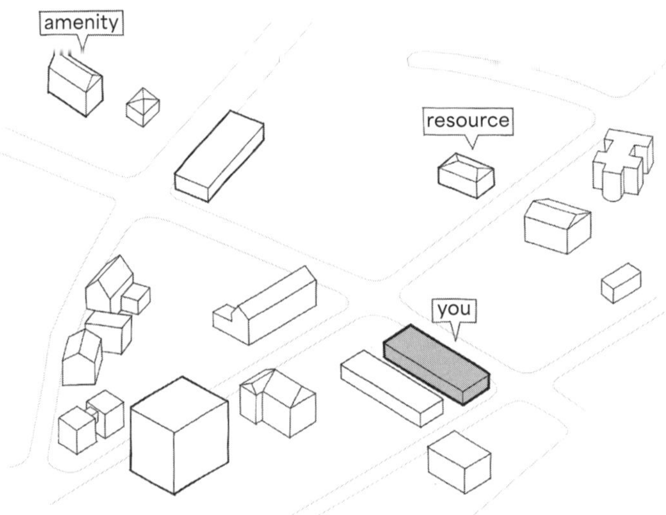

Zoom out to discover what's nearby

New York City, I had a glass desk. Some might say it looked sleeker than a wood desk, but New York gets cold in the winter, and so does glass. If your apartment or office has floor-to-ceiling windows like mine did, you might not want to sit down to work because you hate the feeling of sitting at a cold desk.

The decision of what material the desk should be isn't one you make in isolation. You must *zoom out* to consider how the wider environment affects your or others' experience using the design.

Here's another example. Say you're trying to figure out where to place electrical outlets. If you adhere to standard practices, you may evenly space a couple of outlets on each wall at a certain height above the floor, like the code requires. Later, as you bring in furniture and install cabinetry, you may realize that some of the outlets are blocked or are difficult to reach because you hadn't considered their relationship to the furniture and cabinetry.

If you were to do this exercise again, this time zooming out to think about what else will be in the room and how people are meant to use it, you might design the space differently. You might end up with outlets that aren't blocked by furniture and are better positioned—like above rather than below countertops and desks—so that people can easily reach them.

We can keep zooming out past the scale of a room to consider an even broader context.

Let's say you're designing a house and deciding where to locate a bedroom to optimize sleep. To find the best location, it's not just a matter of looking at the bedroom's location relative to the hallway, bathroom, and other rooms. You also need to *zoom out* and look beyond the house because the house interacts with the street, the buildings nearby, and the activities outside. By zooming out, you may realize that to create the best environment for sleep, you need to orient the bedroom away from the busy street or noisy areas outside the house.

Of course, not every design element interacts with every other element in its vicinity. The material of your kitchen cabinets probably won't affect the flooring's performance too much. But by not zooming out at all, you will miss important information about how various aspects of your design threaten or support one another.

Zoom out teaches us that something as seemingly innocuous as the temperature of a lightbulb, the color of a wall, or the material of a desk can have far-reaching consequences in the context of the overall design. It's always in your interest to *zoom out* because more data is better for making a well-informed decision.

Imagine what might happen if you were to act without all the data. Maybe you buy a house because when you visited during the day, you really liked the interior—the large rooms, the high ceilings, and the flow through

Something as seemingly innocuous as the temperature of a lightbulb, the color of a wall, or the material of a desk can have far-reaching consequences in the context of the overall design.

the home. Then you start living there and begin discovering all these annoying qualities—loud neighbors blasting their music into the night, a train rumbling by every thirty minutes, a light from a nearby store that beams into your bedroom. At this point you realize that you considered the house in only one context: during the day, at the exact time when you took the tour. You didn't *zoom out* to understand the full context at other times of day.

Save yourself headaches (and some money too). Practice the Baaham principle of *zoom out* early and often, and gather data about the context of the space before making decisions.

Even at the municipal level, it's imperative to *zoom out.* A lot of agencies in the government influence construction projects: planning and zoning, building, fire, water, transportation, and more. Sadly, because they don't regularly think beyond their department to the broader concerns of a community, their efforts often impede (rather than benefit) our ability to create healthy and life-giving places.

Recently, I was designing a building where certain government officials expressed a desire to create a more vibrant, walkable city. But their colleagues in the planning department and fire department were not on the same page. Since the city's planning codes required our building to be set back at least ten feet from the sidewalk, the street it was on felt suburban and empty. Because the transportation department hadn't built continuous sidewalks and allowed roads to have high speed limits, walking felt unsafe. The fire department was so worried about the type of fire that could happen once in a thousand years that the city's buildings had to be far apart from one another, so the distance to get from place to place became greater. Without *zoom out*, the people in these agencies couldn't see the problems they were causing. Their siloed efforts were creating a future public health crisis: The city wasn't walkable, and driving was the only option, increasing the chances that residents would lead sedentary lives and face greater risks for obesity and chronic disease.[1]

HOW TO ZOOM OUT

To practice *zoom out*, we must dedicate time and energy to thinking about the design in a holistic sense. How do the various elements in the space interact with one another and the people using the space? How does the space interact with the context surrounding it? Several techniques are available to help us answer these questions.

Mindshift: Think about location and use

Zoom out doesn't just allow you to see relationships between individual design elements. It lets you revisit the purpose of your entire project so you can design with the most appropriate furniture, lighting, materials, technology, and even equipment like your HVAC system.

When choosing a paint color, for instance, *zoom out* past the wall and think about the purpose of that space. The color you pick can affect people's moods and performance in the room. For example, because blue is the most common color in the world, a wall painted blue can give people a feeling of calm, comfort, and safety.[2] Meanwhile, dark-colored walls may improve someone's experience having dinner because the surroundings get muted, allowing the person to focus on the meal in front of them.

Color, in other words, isn't purely a matter of taste; it's not neutral in the

To practice *zoom out*, we must dedicate time and energy to thinking about the design in a holistic sense.

design. It will affect people in certain ways, so it's better to consider those effects than to ignore them or choose a color arbitrarily.

Lighting is another design element that's easily overlooked but affects people's experience in a space by interacting with other elements. When selecting lights, people tend to think about the decorative aspect of the fixture more than the bulb, but even small changes in color temperature (kelvins), brightness (lumens), and location can dramatically change people's feelings and performance.[3]

For example, researchers have found that cool lighting (temperatures between 4500 and 6000 kelvins) may stimulate more concentration on tasks, while warmer lighting (3000 kelvins) may stimulate more creative thinking.[4] Before you choose, think beyond the light and identify what needs to happen in that space. Is it a space for relaxing or working? Do you want the space to help you focus or let your mind wander? These answers will tell you what kinds of lights and what arrangements of those lights will best suit the space.

As a final example, consider how the location of your design affects the way people use it—if they use it at all. In many airports and hospitals, for example, have you noticed exhibits of art or history displayed in the hallways? While the intent is to have people stop and look at something interesting, that effect is rarely achieved because people don't tend to stop in hallways. They walk. And if they were to pause to look, they would block traffic because there isn't sufficient space.

Now consider how many more people would see the exhibits if they were placed in the seating and lounge areas. But you only realize that by zooming out to think about the relationship between the art, the location it's in, and how people use the space.

Practice: Coordinate across trades and disciplines

If your project requires professionals from different disciplines, communication must exist between the various teams throughout the project's duration. A good way to do this is to set up coordination meetings between disciplines, where, for example, the lighting designer meets with the graphic designer, the graphic designer meets with the furniture designer, and the furniture designer meets with the electrical engineer. Each of these people should also meet in a group setting so they can present their designs and everyone can see how the various elements will work together.

This will also prompt each designer and engineer to give feedback on whether the current design serves their needs and, if not, how it could be modified to work with their disciplines better. For instance, a furniture designer could point out to the interior designer and electrical engineer that the workbenches in the laboratory room are thirty-four inches tall, so the outlets on that wall would be better placed, and more functional, if they were placed above the surface of the bench (thirty-four inches) rather than at the standard height near the floor. This conversation would help the electrical engineer *zoom out* beyond his or her own discipline and think about the context for the outlet locations.

With so many people involved in the creation of our built environment, quality conversations and an understanding of what others are doing are key to building well.

Practice: Observe and study the context

Whether you're designing a single room or an entire city block, you're not designing against a blank slate. You need to understand the dynamics of how the place works, how people behave, and how your intervention might affect the status quo.

One of my earlier projects was designing a new psychotherapy clinic in the heart of New York City. It was in one of the busiest neighborhoods in one of the world's busiest cities. The clinic was going to be in a suite on the building's tenth floor. As I was beginning to design the clinic, I had a crucial realization that involved zooming out to consider the context. I zoomed out past the tenth floor, past the clinic's suite, and realized that because the building was in the middle of Manhattan—a place so rushed, with so much hustle and bustle—patients could easily feel like they had no opportunity to reflect before their session or once it was over.

To avoid this experience, I designed the clinic so people could leave their sessions and make use of an individual pod for five to ten minutes of reflection and quiet. Each pod has images of greenery and plays soothing music. This design element wouldn't have made as much sense in a quieter rural area, where it's not so go, go, go. But in hectic New York City, zooming out past the clinic and considering the broader context allowed me to improve people's experience in that location.

Practice: Walk through the design

Before anything is built, you'll want to immerse yourself in a virtual version of the design. If you're the client, ask your designer to show you the design in virtual reality or 3-D modeling software.[5] If you're the designer, make it a priority to fully render the design for the people who will be using the space so they can see their design "at work" before the project advances any further. By "fully render," I don't mean simply showing them the details of the finishes or materials. If you've designed a kitchen, don't just show people a 3-D rendering of blank marble countertops. That won't give them a sense of what it will be like to use the space. Instead, render the countertops with all the appliances that will sit on the counter and take up space. That way, they can see how much space is left over, and together, you can decide if it's enough to suit their needs. Do this with each part of the design, "walking through" the virtual model and looking around. Examine how the different elements interact with one another and whether each can serve its purpose.

This method has saved me numerous times. For instance, it helped me catch an Exit sign that would have obstructed someone's view of a projector screen. Someone had selected the sign without fully thinking about the context, so the sign's hanging stems were in the line of sight of people looking at the screen. We wouldn't have caught this issue if we hadn't taken the time to walk through the design before making it real.

More than still images and renders (and definitely more than wall or floor plans), 3-D–model walk-throughs will help you think about people's experience with the design elements in a space and how those elements are meshing with their surroundings.

Practice: Ask for peer review

To get a fuller picture of how your design may work in practice, search for a second opinion. If you're designing for yourself, ask a friend or family member who knows you well. If you're designing for someone else, ask another professional, much like a scientist seeking a peer review.

You aren't asking for their opinions about style or taste. Instead, you're asking about functionality. This will get them to think about the performance of the design elements in the surrounding context. If you ask a couple different people, they may consider different aspects of the context and help you make more thoughtful design decisions.

Mindshift: Consider unintended consequences

Not everyone who is affected by the design will be using the space per se. Some people are affected because they live or work *near* the design. And some are affected because the design disrupts an ecosystem that people in the space depend on. So ask yourself, *Who or what might be inadvertently affected by this design?*

Let's say I'm designing a tall building in a city. Even if I think I have the perfect design for the exterior and interior, down to the finest details, what if I fail to consider that there's a park on the block next to this building? The families who use the park and the kids who play on its playground aren't direct stakeholders like the employees who go to work in the building each day, but they are affected nonetheless. If the building casts a shadow that makes the park gloomy and unpleasant, then I've done the community a disservice by creating a building that negatively impacts those groups.

Ancillary groups need to be considered when designing, not just the people who will be using the space. Even if the design is good for the occupants, if it's bad for animal ecosystems or the environment, the project will ultimately be bad for humans. Remember that.

PUTTING IDEAS INTO PRACTICE

Designers around the world have applied *zoom out* to great success. Take the 1896 waterfront house in Trincomalee, Australia, located twenty-five miles north of Sydney. The home was built with many small and medium-sized design features that were all considered together, as part of a unified design, rather than in isolation.

For instance, the home's fireplace was created in service of promoting conversation. Known as an inglenook fireplace, it's recessed into a nook in the wall and includes two built-in benches facing one another. This allows you to sit beside the fireplace and not just enjoy its warmth but also have an intimate conversation under a low ceiling that embraces you as you sit in the nook. By considering what the room needed, the designer created a fireplace that went from offering one function (heat) to two (heat and a cozy place to sit).

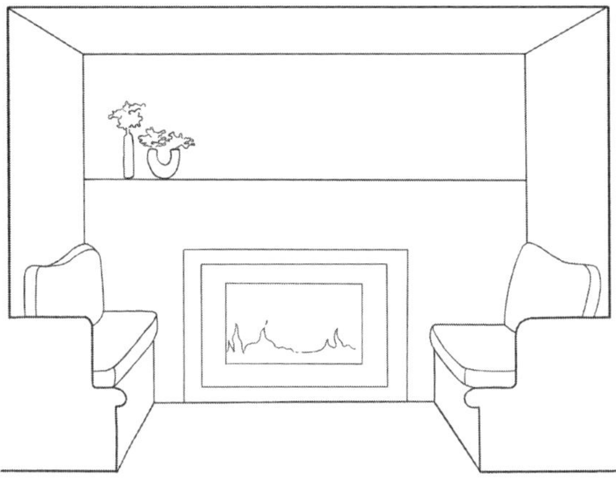

Around the house, flooring was designed in a similar way—chosen based on its context. In rooms meant to be quieter, like the family and reading rooms, there's carpet to dampen noise. In the sunroom, wooden flooring absorbs heat and shares it with your bare feet as you're seated or walking across the room. In both cases, the design element was considered in its broader context—the room it's in—and what the experience of the room needed to be.

Windows represent a third case of zooming out to consider the broader context. No windows were placed at random. They were carefully positioned to frame the best views of the waterfront and surrounding landscape—an act of zooming out that recognized that the windows' role in the house isn't just to bring in light but also to frame views of the outdoors that make you feel immersed in the natural landscape and promote a sense of awe.

With each detail, the design of the Trincomalee house reinforces a sense of warmth and welcome—an aspect of the design that could be created only by thoughtfully zooming out.

+ + +

Zoom out is the final principle of Baaham in the scope of this book, but it shows up in all phases of design. It should become second nature in your design process whenever you're deciding what kinds of spaces are necessary and what kinds of elements will make up the design.

To start zooming out, ask yourself: *How does what I'm designing fit within its context?*

REVISITING THE PRINCIPLES OF BAAHAM

As we wrap up part 2, let's revisit the principles of Baaham to see how each helps you create the best design possible.

- **Look within.** Learn as much as you can about the people for whom you're designing: what motivates them, what they need, and how the space can serve them best.
- **Solve important problems.** Remember that design is principally a process for removing obstacles to people's desired experiences, not turning a profit, chasing status, or appealing to the latest trends.
- **Design for change.** Nudge people toward helpful mindsets and behaviors while keeping in mind how the space can evolve over time to suit people's changing needs.
- **Follow nature.** Ensure that your design supports people's biological rhythms through sunlight, airflow, openness, stimulation, and exposure to nature.

- **Embrace details.** Pay attention to the finer aspects of your design that determine both how the design works and whether its visual aesthetic creates the desired feeling in the space.
- **Build ecologically.** Rely on local materials and solutions to promote sustainability in your design and to make the space beloved and worth protecting.
- **Zoom out.** Consider the context surrounding your design, and make each element of your design work together.

When we adhere to these principles, we can design spaces that give people beneficial experiences, that help people achieve their goals, and that help people become who they aspire to be. On the following page, you'll find the full collection of Baaham principles and their guiding questions, which you can refer to whenever you're starting a new project.

As we will see in part 3, whether it's for living, working, learning, healing, or coexisting within a community, Baaham is the way to design the world we want for ourselves.

BAAHAM DESIGN CANVAS

LOOK WITHIN

Who am I designing for, and what do they need from their space?

SOLVE IMPORTANT PROBLEMS

What's the most important goal this space needs to achieve?

DESIGN FOR CHANGE

How do I want to nudge people through this design? What will allow the space to adapt over time?

FOLLOW NATURE

What biological needs should this space meet for people?

BUILD ECOLOGICALLY

What local solutions already exist for my project type? How will I minimize environmental impact?

EMBRACE DETAILS

What finer points must I not lose sight of while designing? How can I make this space beautiful?

ZOOM OUT

How does what I'm designing fit within its context?

PART 3

BAAHAM IN ACTION

Building great places is challenging–there are hurdles of cost, timelines, egos, regulations, and feasibility. But the world we can have with Baaham is incredible and worth fighting for. This section shows what's possible if we stop thinking incrementally and muster the courage to move beyond our perceived limitations–if we dare to dream of what we really want.

12

DESIGN FOR BETTER LIVING

A home is far more than a shelter. It reflects who we are and influences who we become.

HOMES THAT SUPPORT PEACE AND SECURITY

We spend more time in our homes than anywhere else, which means their design affects our health, well-being, relationships, thoughts, and feelings more than any other space. Whether we rent or own, whether we live in an apartment building or a single-family home, whether we live alone or with a roommate, a partner, children, pets, or an aging parent, our home is an anchor and an influence.

Great homes support us in living the ways we want, whether it's waking up early, practicing healthy habits, or spending quality time with family. They are ideal environments for resting, cleansing, cooking, and sometimes, expressing ourselves through work and creative passions. We also expect our homes to be places of refuge. Home represents a haven from a chaotic, uncontrollable world. Our homes help us feel like we belong somewhere. If nowhere else in the world, we can at least go home.

Great homes support us in living the ways we want, whether it's waking up early, practicing healthy habits, or spending quality time with family.

In this chapter, we'll focus on the type of living space with which many people are familiar: the single-family home.

CURRENT REALITY

Most of our homes aren't designed to support our lives to the fullest. There are many reasons for this.

For starters, estimates suggest that for the past few decades, somewhere between 75 and 90 percent of buildings in America have been built without an architect, including homes.[1] Because providing housing has morphed into the business of real estate, many of the homes developed today are created in the fastest way possible. For homeowners, that often means working directly with the builder and skipping the architect. For builders, it means using shortcuts like cheap materials and shoddy construction practices. The result is that homes are built without anyone spending much time or thought on the design.

Even when we're presented with options that may be better, we've been miseducated to choose poorly for ourselves. Maybe we're overly concerned with what others will think of our homes instead of focusing on what we want and need. We may look around and ask, "What is everyone else doing?" and make decisions about our homes that help us fit in and get approval from others.

For instance, we've been taught to think about resale value to such a degree that we might forget we're going to live in the home for years or decades before trying to capture any selling value. This may lead us to include features in our homes that are never used, like a formal dining room, just because it may lead to selling the home faster and at a higher markup—if we eventually decide to sell. Never mind that we personally have no use for it.

These choices degrade our quality of life.

Noise and light from the streets outside make it harder to sleep at night. The walls and windows are so thin that we hear every car driving by, conversations on the street, sirens in the distance. With blinds instead of proper shutters or blackout shades, it's hard to get our bedrooms fully dark so we can rest peacefully in a cavernous environment like our ancient ancestors did. With little thought given to where our bedrooms face relative to the street and what materials are used, we wake up in the morning more sluggish than we deserve.

Even cooking is harder than it needs to be. With poorly laid out kitchens, we may find ourselves maneuvering around our partners during the morning rush or bumping into one another while cooking dinner. Most of us are breathing contaminated air in our kitchens as well. A proper exhaust hood above a stove vents air out of the house. But in many modern homes, the hood is purely decorative. When you turn on the fan, the buildup from the stove just gets blown around the room. No air is vented out of the house. In our bathrooms, though they seem standard, the problems may lie with what we accept as standard. With toilets so high, we're positioned in unnatural postures while trying to do our business.

Even the home's promise of protecting us from the elements isn't fully fulfilled. In warm weather, many people's upstairs floors begin to bake. Their homes lack the proper roof overhangs, awnings, window recesses, shutters (that aren't merely decorative), and trees that could shield the house from the hot sun. Even with the AC blasting, we're not always comfortable or able to cover up bad design.

Our furniture, too, is often poorly designed for optimal comfort. Many of our couches are designed for six-foot-two Scandinavians rather than for the average American, who's several inches shorter. Their seats are often too deep, so many of us slouch instead of sitting upright, leaving us with weaker backs and unexplained aches and pains.

Our minds and emotions also suffer. In other rooms, family members or roommates make noises while we're trying to read or write or sleep, and we get upset with them (not realizing it's in part because our walls lack insulation to dampen noise). It's difficult to find peace and quiet when our houses were so poorly designed.

In the end, our homes are merely decent when we need them to be great.

PREPARING FOR YOUR BAAHAM HOME

Whether you're designing your own Baaham home or a home for someone else, whoever is going to live in the space should be the focus of your design. They are your target.

Let's say you're designing your own home. At the start, designing your Baaham home is all about reflection—on what you need and how you want to live. Don't worry about what others are doing in their homes. Your home should be an extension of you. To help you reflect, ask: *What do I wish was better about my home? What doesn't work so well?* Think through one space at a time. Literally go stand in your kitchen and look around. Picture yourself using the space, and imagine what annoys you. Is it hard to reach pots and pans? Is it impossible to keep an eye on the stove while prepping ingredients? Scrutinize every part of the space, making note of what could be better. Then walk to your bedroom, bathroom, and other rooms, and perform the same exercise—ideally with your family members tagging along to offer their thoughts.

Next, consider how you want to live. Write down the type of person you want to be, the things you want to prioritize. Maybe you want to become a healthier person who reads a lot and pursues creative hobbies. Jot down the aspirational traits you wish to embody because your home can help you achieve them.

For the next few days, observe your life. Assess how your space helps or hurts your ability to be the type of person you want to be. Is the way food is stored in your kitchen influencing the kind of diet you keep? Does the bedroom lighting make it easy to read at night? Do you have enough space for your creative projects? Does your living room layout steer you to watch TV rather than have conversations with your family? Track the ways your home is either supporting or hindering you.

With these lists of priorities and problems, you're ready to put pen

Designing your Baaham home is all about reflection—on what you need and how you want to live.

to paper and start designing a Baaham space, whether you're remodeling your existing home or building a brand-new one.

As you embark, question any assumptions you have for how the design "should" look. For example, if you think you want a sleigh bed in your bedroom, ask yourself why. If you want a certain countertop material in the kitchen, question that too. Bring your focus to what you want to achieve—who you want to be—rather than which finishes or what kind of look catches your eye. Deciding the proper finishes and overall look will be important eventually but not this early in the process.

For now, design a space that makes your life easy. Eliminate the frictions you currently experience. Design nudges that encourage you to make smarter choices and that help you become who you want. Your nudges can be as small as displaying apples in your favorite room so you eat more fruit or lowering your bed so you use your leg muscles more.

More involved nudges could include building a reading room with comfy seating near sunlight, so you're drawn to read. Or keeping the living room far from the kitchen so that, at dinnertime, your family sits around the table to eat and talk. And when you're finally at your local hardware store or furniture showroom shopping for your home, remember what you're trying to achieve with your design. Instead of picking what looks good in-store, pick what works well for the life you want. Understand how you want to live, and let the design flow from there.

A VISION FOR BAAHAM HOMES

If you follow Baaham, here's one example of how your home could feel.

Your morning begins well-rested and tranquil, just as you deserve. You slept in silence all night because your bedroom faces away from the street, and your walls are soundproof thanks to densely packed straw insulation. You didn't hear a peep from outside.

Rising from your bed, which sits only a foot off the ground, you propel yourself up using your legs and hips, which have gotten stronger and more limber from the daily squatting into and out of bed. While your partner sleeps, you walk across the bedroom over noise-free flooring. You pass under an arched, cave-like ceiling that is designed to move heat away from the bed so you stay cool while you sleep. Then you climb five steps that take you out of your bedroom. The climbing further activates your muscles, waking your body and signaling to your brain that it's time to start the day, as if rising out of a cave. You silently close the squeak-free door so that your partner, who wakes up an hour after you, can remain undisturbed.

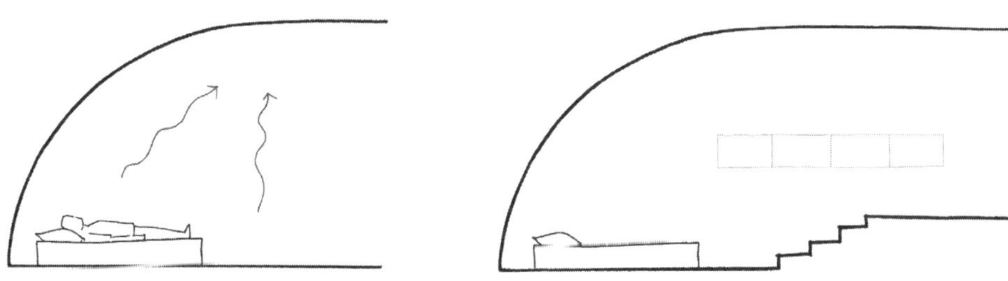

Just outside the bedroom is a hallway that leads to the closet and then the bathroom. In the hallway is a shelf where a filled water bottle awaits you. After eight hours of sleep, your body is dehydrated, and the placement of the water bottle nudges you to drink water right when you need it the most. You chug sixteen ounces of water and make your way toward the bathroom.

Located past the closet, farther from the bedroom, the bathroom is cleverly positioned to prevent the noise of a running shower or flushing toilet from disturbing your sleeping partner. So the order of rooms goes quietest, noisier, noisiest.

In the bathroom, a well-positioned window lets sunlight stream in and hit your eyes, fully waking you up. You stand in front of the mirror, whose lighting is soft and warm, and this accentuates your skin tone and overall appearance, filling you with confidence to start the day.

As you leave the bathroom, you turn and walk into a glass-enclosed greenhouse that connects to the louder side of the home, with the kitchen and family room. Under the glass, you spend a few minutes stretching and watering your cilantro plant. Seeing this much natural light early in the day kick-starts your energy and improves your mood. It's also rebooting your circadian rhythm, and a healthy circadian rhythm means you'll enjoy better sleep, balanced hormones, and improved physical and mental health. You'll probably live longer too.

You finish stretching and head inside to the kitchen to make breakfast for the family. With enough countertop space, you're able to spread out and comfortably prepare everyone's food. The kitchen's layout also lets you keep your eye on the stove while chopping fruits and gathering ingredients. Everything is right where you want it to be.

To promote healthier eating, nutritious snacks are stored on the counter and in the open shelving, while the treats you want to eat more sparingly are hidden in tins at the back of the lower cabinets.

As the family pours into the kitchen, chasing the smell of the breakfast you've made, they grab some fruit and healthy side items, since those are easy to see, and tuck into the comfy breakfast nook that's surrounded by a big bay window on three sides. Because humans are phototropic—that is, drawn to light and affected on emotional and physiological levels by light exposure—this sunny nook makes you comfortable. Outside, you can see your courtyard and garden—views of nature that offer therapeutic benefits year-round. On nice days, you open the sliding doors and take your coffee and sit outside. Your morning has a sense of calm, not rush.

Nourished and energized, you're ready to get started on work. You're working mostly from home today, so you make your way into your study. Having your own space in the house makes life easier since you can arrange it just as you want. It's your sanctuary for solitude. The walls are thickened by closets and bookshelves, so you're protected from noises in the rest of the house and can work unbothered. The low ceiling and greenish-blue walls—which have natural imperfections from lime wash paint—are calming and make it easier to focus.

Midway through the day, you walk from the study out to the courtyard garden you share with your neighbors to find a shady spot. Here you are unencumbered by ceilings, leaving your mind free to float and wander and entertain new ideas as they arrive. The natural scene before you allows your vision to soften on the hedges, trees, shrubs, and flowers. In your study, your computer screen was inches from your face. Here your vision can "stretch its legs" as you gaze far into the distance, perceiving the birds and other wildlife but not really focusing on any of it.

In this outdoor working environment, you find yourself free to make connections that you never seemed to notice before. With your notebook beside you, you jot down some of the ideas that bubble up. You feel maximally creative, and you can't wait to share your best ideas with your coworkers when you meet later today.

Even though it's the middle of a summer day, you're feeling comfortable both outside and inside the house. The trees outside offer ample shade and keep the ambient temperature cooler. Windows on opposite walls let fresh breezes pass through. The roof on your house is painted white to reflect sunlight away. It also overhangs by six feet, protecting the house's exterior from sun (while providing you a covering to walk under on rainy days).

On the house's south side, recessed windows and awnings minimize how much sun hits the glass, keeping the inside cooler. On days like this, you're happy you decided to add a solar chimney facing the sun because it heats up and sucks hot air out of the house so that cooler fresh air can enter through low windows. (Plus, in the winter, you can shut the top of the chimney so as the sun heats it up, hot air from the chimney enters the house, warming you for free.)

In the afternoon, you walk to a work meeting not far from your home. You work there the rest of the day, and as you're arriving home, you see your partner and kids in the gazebo-like structure attached to the front of the house, reading books on the benches. It's a semi-enclosed outdoor space that creates connection with the street and neighborhood but still offers privacy. And it's a place where everyone can gather and feel connected to the hum of a vibrant neighborhood. Your family greets you with wide smiles and big hugs as you all walk inside.

It's just about time for dinner now. While your partner preps the food, you and the kids head into the garden to pluck some peas and zucchini. In addition to giving everyone tranquil views of nature, the garden serves as a way to teach your kids about agriculture and nutrition. There they learn about growing crops, witness different plants growing, and build habits they'll look back on fondly as they get older. Plus, tending to the garden offers the whole family a gentle form of exercise and gets everyone outside. Once everything is prepared, your family sits down at the table, which is shaped like a circle so that there is no head of the table and each person is recognized as a valued member of the whole.

After the family finishes dinner, food scraps are tossed in a composter, and everyone migrates to the family room. The layout is carefully designed to create alcoves and niches that give people their own spaces without sacrificing a feeling of togetherness. There are low couches (slightly taller than your bed) in the center of the room for gathering while at the edges are various games, activities, and seating for people to stay entertained in their own ways, without being separated from the family. At first, you're playing a board game with your kids while your partner reads on the couch. Later, you join your partner while your kids continue to play in the nearby alcoves. Even though everyone is doing different things, you're all together, enjoying one another's company.

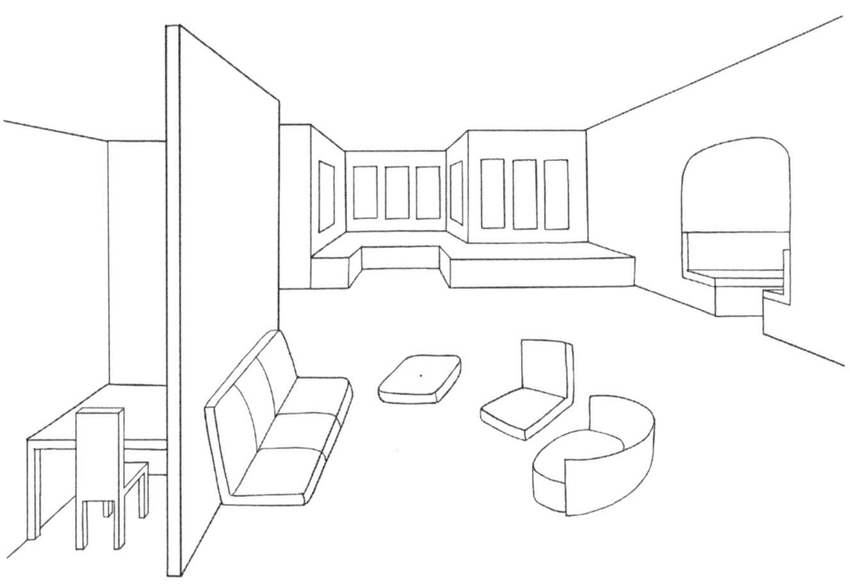

As the sun goes down, you make your way to the bathroom to wash up before bed. Notice how there are two light switches in your bathroom. One controls the morning light, the other the evening light. The morning light is brighter and cooler, which mimics daylight. The evening light is dimmer and tinted amber, the same hue as a sunset, which cues your body that it's time for sleep. And if you make a trip to the bathroom at some point in the night, the amber light doesn't shock you awake, so you can quickly return to a deep sleep.

Leaving the bathroom, you descend the steps back into your bedroom, back toward slumber. The arched ceiling and walls are now dark—a special paint shifts the walls from bright in the morning to wake you up to dark at night to help you sleep. This effect makes it feel like you're entering a cave for sleep. Your body is ready to fall into bed. While your partner falls asleep quickly, you need help. So you look up at the ceiling at an angled skylight that shows you the stars. Staring into space, you drift off to a deep sleep.

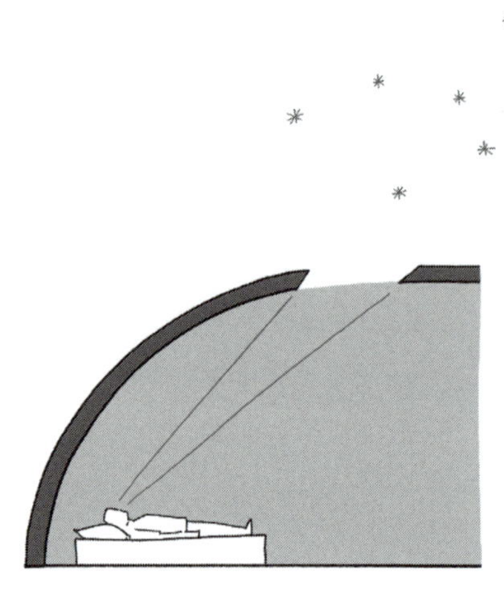

It's a beautiful life, made possible with Baaham design.

This vision for Baaham homes can be adjusted to suit your life and goals. Perhaps you want to live a bit differently. Maybe you want to increase intimacy with your partner or improve the relationship with your kids or spend more time alone pursuing your hobbies. The promise of a Baaham home is that all people feel fully supported, equipped, and empowered to live the lives they choose because their days start and end with a home that supports them in those ways.

As philosopher Alain de Botton has pointed out, "We are, for better or for worse, different people in different places," and "it is architecture's task to render vivid to us who we might ideally be."[2] That is to say, certain homes reinforce our best habits and make us healthier and happier versions of ourselves, while some homes make it nearly impossible for us to live well and in the ways we want.

A Baaham home is one that's designed to reinforce all the good things while minimizing the bad. Your better life starts with a Baaham home.

13

DESIGN FOR BETTER WORKING

A great office supports our ongoing needs for learning, development, and creative potential.

OFFICES THAT NOURISH MIND, BODY, AND SPIRIT

While some envision a time when robots will do our work and we'll lead lives of leisure, working remains a source of fulfillment and meaning for so many people, whether it's their careers, volunteer efforts, or personal projects. Work is what offers many of us a sense of achievement and purpose. It seems unlikely that work is going away anytime soon.

On average, full-time American workers spend close to one-third of their lives working. So it's vital to pay attention to the places where so much of life unfolds.

In ideal circumstances, our workplaces are distraction-free so we can focus and fulfill our responsibilities, not places that cause friction, slowing us down and making us spend more time at work than we need to. They should be places specifically designed around work, providing what we need to get into and maintain a state of flow.

In this chapter, we're focusing on office spaces because that's where a significant portion of people work these days, whether it's a corporate office, coworking space, or home office. The best offices are places that help us achieve our goals, supporting us in becoming the best intellectual and professional versions of ourselves—while also connecting us with others, meeting our biological needs, and giving our minds and bodies a break when needed.

CURRENT REALITY

Offices today rarely live up to this ideal. That's because offices, especially corporate offices, are often designed through a flawed process: The project objectives are perverse, the people involved aren't in alignment, and the space's occupants aren't properly considered.

The best offices are places that help us achieve our goals, supporting us in becoming the best intellectual and professional versions of ourselves.

For starters, many offices in America are built by speculative real estate developers. They invest money in a project and look to fill it with tenants to earn back their money plus a profit. The best way to do this, they often believe, is to make a building that looks great from the outside. They attract tenants with curb appeal, not necessarily by making a design that leaves workers happy and satisfied.

Even when organizations design their own offices, they tend to make a similar mistake. To attract talent or shout their arrival to the world, they overfocus on creating office spaces that appear impressive at first glance rather than on places that care for and nurture workers.

I have a dear friend who works for a company that, a few years ago, created a new headquarters that became a media darling for its stunning shape and visual appeal. But as my friend tells me, the experience of working there doesn't live up to the hype.

Actually, she says the office is terrible.

She says it doesn't feel like the designers consulted any women while designing. The temperature inside is constantly too cold. The bathrooms are too far away. The lack of privacy makes it difficult to focus and get work done. Even the cafeteria is so inconveniently located that she often doesn't have time to get all the way there for lunch.

Workplaces are designed like this for several reasons. In many cases, organizations feel the need to show off. They think that splashing their logos and brand colors everywhere will stir up feelings of loyalty and dedication among staff. That's why so many people are subjected to sitting in rooms splashed with harsh colors that don't help them focus and often send them home with a headache.

In other cases, offices fail their occupants because the architects and interior designers haven't internalized the true purpose and goals of the space. For them, the office's design isn't about making it easier for employees to focus, create, and collaborate—it's about making the office look cool and trendy and designing something that looks good in their portfolios and in the media.

But then again, how could they design a space that meets people's needs? Workers are rarely consulted when offices are being built. Because the thinking is often narrow—more focused on flash and appeal than on function or support—many offices in America feel outdated and incapable of supporting the way people need to work today. During the design process, not enough thought was given to the future—the occupants, their needs, the state of the organization—or to creating an office that can adapt with the changing times.

When the process for designing offices has so many missteps, you (the worker) suffer. Sometimes the inconveniences are mild, such as outlets placed too close to the floor, so you're getting down on all fours just to plug in a device. Other times, the poor design does more harm. You feel like there's not the right space for the way you like to work, so you're unable to perform your best. Or the office is designed to be either too social or too isolating, which can be draining for you based on your personality. At the same time, the modern office is full of distractions. People shuffling near you. The sound of traffic outside the building. A coworker humming. People having meetings that you can hear, even though you don't want to. It's difficult to focus. Your productivity slows down. The task you were working on is now going to take you longer to finish, so you're going to spend more hours working. Your deadline is looming. Anxiety builds.

On top of that, while you're at the office, your health is taking a hit.

You can't control the windows or ventilation system, so it's too cold or too muggy. You're sitting all day, getting sleepy. The bad air quality is making you sick. You don't realize it, but the office is where your head cold originated. The incessant noises and poor lighting are slowly piling up, adding more and more stress. Being indoors most of the day with little connection to the sun or fresh air or anything far away for your eyes to focus on is causing a decline in your mental health. You might blame yourself.

Forget building a career here. It's hard enough just to stay healthy.

PREPARING FOR A BAAHAM OFFICE

We begin designing a Baaham office by educating. It's important to show everyone involved—the organization's leadership, the designers, and the engineers—all the ways architecture can impact the organization.

Designing an office is not about stockpiling features that may look great—such as a painted mural by the entrance—but don't contribute to employee performance or wellness. So we'll start with a conversation on the cognitive and psychological impact of architecture. We'll ask the decision-makers within the organization how they think architecture influences productivity, well-being, and learning. This conversation will help build a shared understanding of the significance of a worker's surroundings.

In the process, this should open leaders' eyes to a not-so-radical idea: An employee's performance isn't purely a matter of skill and work ethic. Our work environment matters too. We shouldn't take dysfunctional environments for granted or assume that all we can do is change ourselves when, in reality, we have agency to change our environments.

Because many organizational leaders are focused on the bottom line, we'll point out the business advantages of having a well-designed office environment: If the office helps people do their jobs better, the organization

We shouldn't take dysfunctional environments for granted or assume that all we can do is change ourselves when, in reality, we have agency to change our environments.

will be more effective and more productive overall. Workers will be in better health because they'll feel more energized at work and take fewer sick days. And efficiently designed buildings will lower the organization's recurring energy bills. Over time, as the organization succeeds, more people will want to work there. It will begin attracting top talent. Good design makes bottom-line sense.

Once everyone is aligned on the importance of the office design, we'll hold a series of workshops to uncover the organization's objectives. We'll discover who they want to become. This step is vital. To truly promote well-being and productivity, we need to understand how employees and teams work and innovate. Only by recognizing how people generate ideas and perform their work (and how they want to improve their performance) can we design a physical space that supports them.

With clarity on where the organization wants to go, we'll then perform sociological observations to learn about its current state. If the organization already has offices, we'll observe workers in action there. *Where are the gaps between the present and the desired future state? What frictions prevent people from working in the ways they prefer?* These observations will inform the nudges that we design into their environment, both to make work easier and to help workers achieve their objectives.

From there, we'll outline the different problems that need solutions. This will involve meeting with employees to learn their preferences for how they work since not everyone produces his or her best under the same conditions. We'll ask ourselves, *How do we design for a diverse spectrum of people and personalities so that all employees—whether they are introverted or extroverted, prefer digital or analog tools, like working alone or with others, are easily disturbed or need liveliness—can feel good at the office?* That is a question we must answer in our Baaham design.

Along the way, we'll ground our designs in research on human nature and biological needs. For instance, we know that coworkers in the same workspace are three times more likely to collaborate than coworkers who work far apart.[1] We also know it's easier for most people to concentrate under cool-colored lighting versus warm lighting.[2] And because offices struggle to adapt to organizational change, we'll solve for this with scenario planning. With help from the organization's leadership, we'll play out different scenarios of how their teams or workflow may change over time and what will happen if they grow, downsize, or relocate.

Even once the Baaham office is open, our process won't end. We'll monitor how the space is being used and whether it's meeting people's needs. With this data, we'll refine the space and continue optimizing because we know the space isn't fixed.

A VISION FOR BAAHAM OFFICES

In knowledge-based organizations, employees' thoughts and ideas drive success, and the staffing costs associated with people's salaries and benefits often account for up to 90 percent of the organization's expenses.[3] In other words, employees are the most precious resource a company can invest in, which includes the physical environment where their work takes place.

In this respect, Baaham offices cater to two broad outcomes: performing well and feeling good. Nearly every positive outcome an office can achieve falls under these two categories, and the two influence one another.

Performing well

To make it easier to perform well, a Baaham office includes many kinds of spaces, which workers can use based on their varying activities, moods, and personalities. Baaham offices are big on choice.

Sometimes, a worker needs a place to be creative—a place that inspires them and *makes* them creative. In our Baaham office, there are areas to work on projects and foster collaboration across teams, and there are rooms for sparking creativity that feel expansive and have high ceilings, which allow people to think.

To enter these creative spaces, workers first pass through a gallery displaying projects by others in the office—a gallery reminding them that they work on a team and that inspiration can come from anywhere. In these creative spaces, different tools are on display to facilitate different kinds of creative work, such as prototyping, sketching, or putting together mood boards and collages. Making these tools visible, instead of storing them in drawers or cabinets, lets workers see what's available to them and possibly kick-starts a train of thought.

Within these spaces, as well as outside, are pace tracks people can follow, such as a courtyard path or even a large square drawn on the ground,

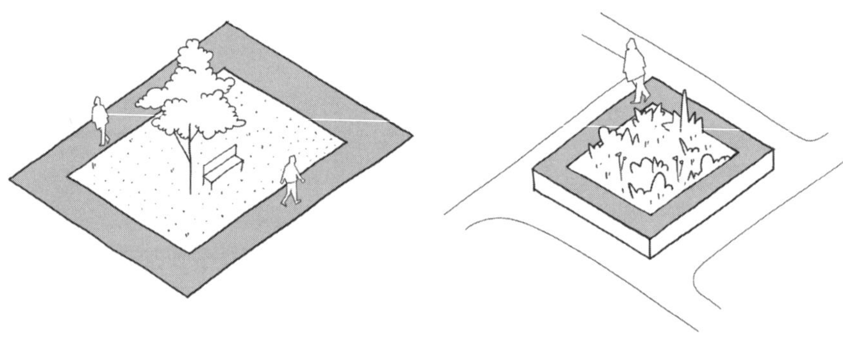

Pace tracks

that allow them to aimlessly pace around. This lets people focus their attention or allow their minds to wander while increasing blood circulation, which is essential for brain function.

Creativity is even nudged at each workstation with sketch pads next to people so they can think with their hands (even if they don't consider themselves to work in a particularly creative role). The sketch pads offer a blank slate for looking at tasks and challenges with fresh eyes. And in areas of the office where people may linger—a lounge, dining area, even a toilet stall—displayed are images depicting the messy early stages of a masterpiece to remind workers not to worry about perfection and just take the first step.

Baaham offices also help workers focus. Our devices and notifications distract us into a state of continuous partial attention, where we're never fully focused on what we're doing, but being effective in our jobs means going beyond shallow work. Baaham offices help people focus their attention so they can experience a flow state and perform deep work.

Because noise is a major cause of distraction, lower cognitive performance, and dissatisfaction, a Baaham office masks and minimizes noises.[4] Walls are fully insulated and thick, and the finishes on the walls, floor, and ceiling further reduce noise by absorbing sounds. Individual workspaces feel partially enclosed with a wall behind and next to the desk, giving workers a sense of separation from distractions. Larger offices may also offer a library space, where workers can go for total peace and quiet. There, the seating is sociofugal, meaning it's designed to discourage interaction and keep the place silent. Some Baaham offices may even offer "flow enclaves," where the space is small and cavernous with a low ceiling, uncluttered walls, nature sounds playing softly, and a shallow depth of field so you can focus on the work in front of you.

Naturally, it's difficult to focus or be creative when you're not feeling comfortable. A Baaham office is a comfortable workplace. Headaches and respiratory issues are minimized because filters and plants continuously clean the air. Windows and ventilation systems are synchronized with carbon dioxide sensors to bring in fresh air to boost cognitive function. Serene color palettes mean your eyes aren't getting tired from staring at stark white walls all day—soft greens and blues are scientifically selected to enhance calm.

When you need more energy, you can head to spaces that have brighter tans and beiges. And because stark office environments can lead workers to feel emotionally exhausted, Baaham offices are detailed to be beautiful: Walls are subdivided into smaller sections with nature-inspired shapes and patterns that put people at ease. Baaham offices also recognize that everyone has different preferences, so the office uses an app that learns what each person likes for lighting, temperature, and ventilation so people can control their spaces.[5] The app also teaches the organization which spaces are most popular among workers so they can create more of those environments.

Offices aren't all about productivity though. The most successful organizations are ones that nurture their employees. They build the right conditions for people to learn and grow so that the organization can innovate and make the biggest possible impact, and Baaham offices accommodate those needs.

Workers can take classes in training halls. They can have meaningful discussions in conversation pits. They can get help from a peer in a cozy nook or observe a senior team member in action in an apprentice-style studio. They can practice their pitch skills on a presentation stage. And because private offices hinder the flow of relationships on a team, individual offices feature an open, triple-wide doorway so teammates feel comfortable popping in for advice and feedback. All this action takes place on wide floors with lots of places for people to run into each other in moments of serendipity, increasing the chances that they will share ideas.

Feeling good

Performing well may be the bottom-line goal of employment, but modern organizations also carry the responsibility to help people feel their best. They understand that performance and well-being are linked. A Baaham office seeks to maximize people's physical, mental, and social well-being and minimize their negative experiences.[6]

Air, light, temperature, sound, water, nature, nourishment, and movement are all incorporated to create a healthy environment. Because greenery and nature are proven to enhance well-being—not to mention creativity and productivity—the office brings plants inside and is organized around views of natural surroundings. Operable windows bring in fresh air. These are combined with angled skylights, which connect workers to the passing of the day and maximize workers' exposure to natural light. Even if the ample natural light needs to be supplemented with electric lights, the lights are bright enough to keep people's circadian rhythms in balance.

To prevent workers from inhaling toxins, the office is constructed from natural, healthy materials that are even capable of cleaning the environment, such as wall paint that uses a process similar to plants to trap harmful substances and molecules suspended in the air.[7] The paint breaks down pollutants into their smallest components, which then evaporate, resulting in pure, fresh air.

Given modern work's emphasis on sitting at a computer and the negative impacts sedentary lifestyles have on our physical and mental health, Baaham offices encourage regular movement. Near each workstation are mirrors, like a fitness center, to help people stay mindful of their posture. Centrally located open stairs encourage workers to move more instead of taking elevators. Along the stairs are trellises filled with fragrant flowers; the smells and new blooms lure people toward a more active way to move between floors.

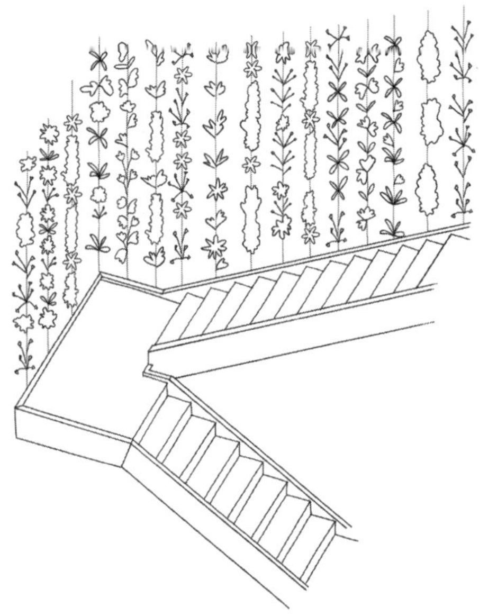

Baaham offices also support people in nourishing their bodies. The office's design nudges them to make healthier decisions overall by featuring healthier snacks at eye level, stowing more indulgent snacks behind frosted glass or in drawers, and posting labels showing the nutritional information of the foods available. And because even mild dehydration can ruin concentration and decrease mood, people can fill up their water bottles at various dispensers around the office.

While workers' bodies will stay healthy, their minds may still need breaks. Around the office, there are many places to take breaks and recharge. Outdoor gardens and courtyards create a lushly vegetated oasis. Employees can sit in the shade of trees and tall plants and listen to water flowing softly over rocks. Because anxiety hinders creative and strategic thinking, the office's green spaces and features like pace tracks are designed to promote a reduction in anxiety, clearing people's minds and resulting in more original thinking.

Inside, people can socialize and decompress in a plaza with food, snacks, and sociopetal lounge seating that orients people to connect with one another. If people prefer to recharge alone, they can hop into a sensory deprivation pod to reset their minds or tuck into a relaxation alcove. In there, they'll have natural soundscapes that promote tranquility and relaxation along with calming, natural scents, such as lavender and bergamot.

Part of feeling good at work is feeling like you're more than a machine whose purpose is to produce and not have any preferences, challenges, or feelings. In a Baaham office, our human side is recognized. For starters, Baaham offices are smaller. Research indicates that in massive buildings, people are less likely to treat others as human and more likely to overlook others and see them as bits in a larger machine.[8] Thus, Baaham offices are smaller and more personal. People arrive and see others as individuals.

In this way, a Baaham office allows people to be themselves. It doesn't lump everyone together. Around a table, the chairs are all different. It seems insignificant—or even like a mistake—but it lets people choose the style of chair they find most comfortable. Soft color palettes, acoustic paneling, and quiet appliances and ductwork minimize sensory overload. All these design choices are meant to help colleagues who are neurodiverse or those who have autism. Baaham offices are also places where families are welcome. To give moms the freedom and dignity to attend to the duties of motherhood, they're given more than small closets for pumping. They're also offered extra space to keep their young kids nearby. These considerations—diverse seating options, minimizing sensory overload, welcoming facilities for mothers—will be lifesavers for a small percentage of people, but they will be welcomed by most everybody.

+ + +

What do you think your relationship with work would be like if you had access to this kind of office environment? Rather than being a stressful or unfulfilling day job with a few bright spots, work might feel genuinely enjoyable on a regular basis. Offices could be places where you have exciting new ideas, challenge your thinking, and achieve great things with your colleagues, specifically because you no longer bear the burden of an ineffective space that makes you sick, distracts you from important tasks, and leaves you feeling emotionally and physically drained.

Designed with Baaham, offices could become great—and go even further. They could become pillars of their communities, much like academic institutions. Instead of shutting down in the evenings, they could reawaken and host a brand-new set of activities supporting the local community. Instead of collecting dust in the corner of an office park, the building could sit closer to the center of the public realm and allow people of all stripes to conduct workshops, host events, train one another, learn skills, and find fellowship as citizens.

Offices may default to places of work in our current conception, but designed with Baaham, they can help entire societies grow and develop together.

14

DESIGN FOR BETTER LEARNING

Education is the most important investment our society can make to ensure its survival.

SCHOOLS THAT NURTURE FUTURE GENERATIONS

In the scope of a person's life, formal education represents just a fraction of time. But those fundamental years are precious because they set you on a trajectory that determines what kind of life you're going to live.

From the first day of kindergarten to the day we complete high school, we spend approximately fifteen thousand hours in school. The only place we might spend more time during this period is at home, which means schools are one of the most important environments for our growth and development. They're where our children are raised to become who they will ultimately be for the world.

The goal we set for education as an institution is a noble one: Develop capable, good humans by endowing them with knowledge, opportunity, and resources and supporting families to increase the chances that their children lead a good life. In this chapter, we will focus on how to use Baaham to make schools that support these goals and turn them into realities.

CURRENT REALITY

Schools are envisioned as places where students can easily learn. Sometimes that means being able to focus, and other times it means being creative, because learning happens in many ways, whether through discussing and debating, researching, observing, ideating, designing, making, or presenting. Schools are meant to support kids no matter which way learning takes place.

Unfortunately, the typical school fails to live up to what we picture for our kids, even as you approach the building from a distance. Because of fears of school shootings, most American schools have visible security:

fences around the campus perimeter, gates and guards, body scanners to pass through when walking in. It feels more like you're walking into a prison than a place to learn.

With so much security, schools are hardly pillars for their communities. In fact, in recent years there's been a growing effort to further separate schools from their communities because elected officials have thought this would make schools safer and protect kids.[1]

This is terribly flawed logic.

The *more* schools are open to the community, the better they serve kids. But because American schools usually have hard boundaries in the form of fences around the perimeter or highly secured entrances, not many community activities are happening there. Even teachers and students are limited in how much they can access their schools with trespassing signs making clear that even they are not allowed at certain hours.

The goal we set for education as an institution is a noble one: Develop capable, good humans by endowing them with knowledge, opportunity, and resources and supporting families to increase the chances that their children lead a good life.

Schools not being open to the public also hurts kids by cutting them off from the real world. They lose a connection to their neighborhoods, their communities, and nature. They sit confined in boxes all day with no sense of what's happening outside or how to interact with the world. It's a sanitized way to grow up. With such emphasis on controlling every aspect of who comes and goes, our schools are greatly underutilized. The average school building in America is being used only one-fifth of the time, which means the current situation leaves schools wasting four-fifths of their chance to serve us.

If you were to assess the point of school, based on the design of a typical American school building, you might conclude that it's a place where we train factory employees. That's because many of America's schools were built in the first half of the 1900s, when the goal was churning out industrial workers.

The schools built during that time are often large, boxlike buildings that contain smaller boxes (that we call "classrooms") connected by straight hallways that shuttle people from one room to the next as efficiently as possible. Within the rooms, desks are arranged in compliant rows facing a teacher so that students—seen as empty heads waiting to be filled with information—can intake what they need to become a cog in an industrial society.

While the goals of education have evolved, the spaces have generally remained fixed. The experience schools want to provide and the spaces they use oftentimes simply aren't in alignment. If we want kids to be critical thinkers, why are they forced to sit in rows and obediently face forward? If we want them to be creative, why are their spaces so uninspiring and lifeless? If we say they are individuals with different strengths and needs, why aren't school spaces differentiated, providing various environments for students to choose from?

This wouldn't be such a problem if schools could easily adapt to changing needs. But because many schools are made of concrete masonry, interior walls end up being structural or otherwise hard to change, so even if the school decides it wants to evolve how it teaches or rethink the kinds of spaces students need, the original structure cannot be changed. The experience can never fully live up to the goal.

Even the inside of a typical classroom is rife with issues: tiny windows that only let in dots of natural light and afford few opportunities for students' eyes to take a break by looking at nature; shiny, reflective floors that create glare and lead to overstimulation; furniture that screeches with every movement; not enough electrical outlets for students; artificial lighting that can cause headaches; noise from HVAC systems, hallways, and adjacent rooms that distract students and muffle voices, leading to learning loss; walls with excessive posters, papers, and decorations that create visual stimuli that younger students can't ignore; and paints, adhesives, furniture, and flooring that are silently releasing toxic gases that kids inhale every day.

If a noisy, chaotic, uninspiring, or toxic design wasn't bad enough, the subliminal message that school buildings can send is even worse. Many schools are crumbling—stained and chipped ceilings, unusable drinking fountains, visible signs of mold—signaling to students that they or their education must not be that important, even if we know the opposite to be true.

PREPARING FOR A BAAHAM SCHOOL

Designing a Baaham school begins with giving special consideration to where the school is situated. That means zooming out to see what the neighborhood has to offer and what it needs. We want to expand the opportunities available to children—not just what their teachers can offer, but what the entire community can offer and teach. What surrounds the school will determine what kinds of spaces will be included in the school's design, so we ask: *What learning experiences can local businesses and organizations provide for students? What kinds of facilities (e.g., medical laboratories, large 3-D printers, performance spaces, etc.) can students access to deepen their learning? What public amenities and infrastructure are available, such as libraries and parks, for students to enjoy?*

By answering these questions (and not assuming we must build something new), we avoid creating redundant facilities that already exist nearby and can be used by the school. Going through this exercise also allows us to survey what the community might be lacking so we can consider adding it on campus to fill a need for local families.

We involve many different groups along the way: students, teachers, faculty, administrators, and parents. Each group has a unique stake in the learning experience that the school delivers, and we want to understand and solve the important problems these groups face. In this process, the teachers, faculty, and administrators are encouraged not to look at or copy what other schools have done or what they see online. Rather, they're asked to reflect deeply on the kinds of experiences they want to create for their students. They're also taken on a tour of other learning spaces, such as libraries, colleges, and vocational training centers so they can experience them firsthand, in action, and so they're prompted to think more deeply about what will work best for their students and what they'd rather leave behind.

By observing and listening to students and teachers, we identify obstacles to learning and can then design an environment that will make the most desirable behaviors the easiest ones to perform. By default, the design will help teachers teach and learners learn. As we begin to imagine how the school itself will be designed, we pay close attention to how well the structure can adapt over time. Education methods are constantly evolving, and the school itself needs to be able to keep up. Modifications must be easy.

Along the way, instead of discussing how well the school colors (which are often arbitrary) can be applied on the hallway walls, lockers, chairs, and signage, we engage our stakeholders in a discussion about the emotional ergonomics of the school's spaces and how to create the right atmosphere for students and teachers.

As various designers on the team explore these details, they coordinate with one another to make sure no decision is made in isolation and could accidentally interfere with another person's design. This includes the architect, interior designer, lighting designer, furniture designer, audiovisual designer, engineers, and more. Not all these people join the project at the beginning, so the architect and educators work together to create a master list of all the criteria that matter. This is a unifying document that gets shared with every designer, engineer, and consultant on the project so that everyone is working to hit the same set of targets.

By observing and listening to students and teachers, we identify obstacles to learning and can then design an environment that will make the most desirable behaviors the easiest ones to perform.

All of this is part of the Baaham process. (You'll notice we haven't discussed any actual design specs yet.) In spaces as complex as schools, where there are dozens of rooms and places for all kinds of activities and where the stakes of getting the overall design right are so high, it's vital that we consider *why* we're building before we think about *what* to build and *how* to build it.

Baaham schools are fundamentally different from traditionally designed schools in this way. They challenge the assumption that schools must be concrete boxes nested within larger boxes and joined by straight lines for efficient processing of students. When we challenge these assumptions and design with a process that includes more perspectives and relevant factors, all of which affect how well students learn, we design schools that transform the educational experience.

A VISION FOR BAAHAM SCHOOLS

At heart, Baaham schools are pillars of their communities.

Maybe that's a neighborhood that spans a few city blocks. Or it could be a well-populated suburb on the outskirts of an urban core. Or a rural town in the countryside. One of the hallmarks of a Baaham school, especially at the scale of its location within a community, is how well it integrates with that community. Students can walk to restaurants to eat lunch, research at the local library, practice at the town's aquatic center, intern at a local company, and use a nearby science laboratory for their projects. The learning opportunities are not just on campus. The entire neighborhood becomes a place where students can learn.

Baaham schools also have amenities that serve local community members based on what people need, such as tech skills training and résumé workshops for career development. These encourage more adults to come on campus and potentially get involved with the school either as a mentor or volunteer. At the very least, they might take an interest in the education process, eventually becoming champions and supporters of the school who can advocate for teachers and students.

Especially ambitious designers and educators may provide housing for senior citizens on the school's campus. In this vision of a Baaham school, senior residents can access the school's amenities and services, and students can volunteer at the senior residence to gain skills in nursing and caretaking, along with administration and operations. As the two groups spend more time together, intergenerational learning begins to take place. Young people learn from community elders and develop greater reverence for past generations, while community elders enjoy longer and healthier lives because they are socializing and cared for. Both seniors and students develop stronger relationships, leading to increased happiness.

This is just one example of Baaham's recognition that academics aren't the only important part of an education. Quality relationships lead to happiness, so Baaham schools feature places for people to hang out, socialize, take breaks, and play. This includes outdoor pavilions and gazebos, fountains and water features, gardens with benches, and game rooms.

Students and teachers can use these facilities to build stronger relationships, especially with people they don't see regularly in class.

To promote wellness within the larger community, Baaham schools are designed so that much of the campus can be accessed after school hours by local residents who wish to use the sports facilities for recreation, the learning spaces for adult education, and the outdoor spaces for movies and local events. Baaham schools may even include "wraparound" services, such as health clinics and food pantries, so that busy parents can run errands in the same spot where they pick up their children. Beyond the logistical benefits, parents who spend more time on campus will feel more inclined to stay involved with the school and their child's education. When schools are reimagined to serve these functions, it's not just students and teachers who benefit, but anyone who wants to feel closer to their community.

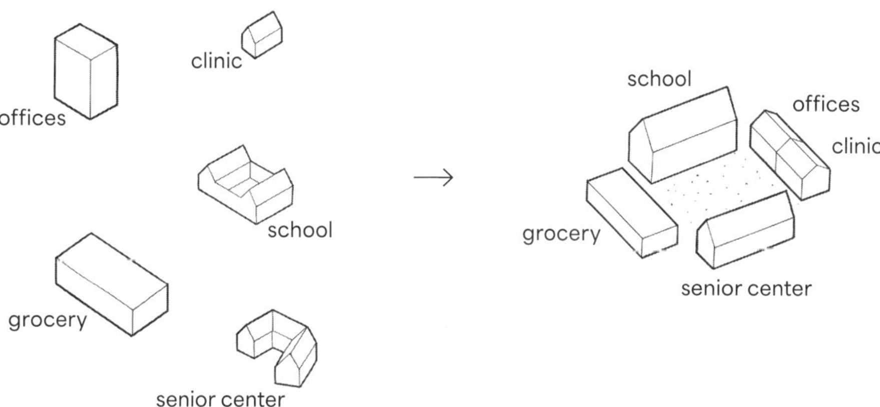

These are just a couple examples of how a Baaham school integrates with its community. There are many more specific design details that education leaders may use to fit their needs and goals.

For example, schools that want to instill entrepreneurial mindsets may consider creating office spaces on campus to host young companies and start-ups. Each week, students can spend a few hours working alongside these professionals, learning about entrepreneurship and helping with various functions of the business, including operations, product design, sales, marketing, and finance. The benefits are symbiotic: While the company receives subsidized (or free) office space for offering this good to the community, the students get hands-on experience learning about business.

A Baaham school can also teach kids how to live ecologically. In this conception, the school itself is built with reclaimed and upcycled materials and highlights these features on walls and furniture so students get in the mindset of reusing things. The school also includes a system for rainwater collection that uses the collected gray water for flushing toilets, for landscaping irrigation, and for watering vegetable gardens that supply produce to the cafeteria.

Along with preserving water, such a Baaham school can compost scraps from leftover food. More advanced design features might include building a butterfly and bee garden, where students can learn about the symbiotic connection between flowers, bees, and butterflies in nature and can produce their own natural products, such as bath or skincare supplies, candles, and other goods from the flowers and honey.

Around the school, sensors for lighting and temperature show how the school consumes and even produces energy. Each of these is in plain view so they can become didactic: By seeing and interacting with these ecological features every day, students come to understand how the building works and start thinking about how to live more ecologically.

However a school decides to situate itself within the larger community, Baaham doesn't judge what's right or wrong. Every community, and every school, is different. What matters is the harmony created between the two so that students are supported in learning what matters most. Even the structure of the school itself is designed to uphold the school as a pillar within its community. Enough care is given so that the outside of the building has visual details that people appreciate, allowing the building to become beloved by locals. Even if one day it's no longer needed as a school, the community will want to keep the beautiful building and reuse it for something else.

While each school may adopt a unique vision for how it connects with its local community, Baaham schools have at least two traits in common within their walls, which remain true no matter the school's size, location, or learning method.

Variety

First, Baaham doesn't assume that classrooms are the default elements that make a school. While they have their benefits for certain kinds of instruction, they don't accommodate other visions of education that may require more creativity, flexibility, and collaboration. Plus, creating variety in the kinds of learning spaces changes how the spaces feel. Kids and teachers won't feel like they're in the same environment all day, and the variations from space to space will make the day less mundane and more fun and will even keep people alert because of the changing stimuli. As students travel between classes, they won't take straight-line pathways, which can make school feel like a grind. Instead, they will have the freedom to take a more meandering path from A to B, which gives them agency over how they travel. Or perhaps they will circulate through larger common areas, where they are free to roam and socialize with other students.

Entering the learning space, the design clearly acknowledges that students learn in all different ways. They each have different preferences for how they learn, how they relax, and how they socialize. That's why, as students settle in to learn, they will encounter a variety of arrangements, atmospheres, and tools. If a child prefers to work alone at times, he can. If another child works best on the floor, she can. Whether the children prefer to work using analog or digital tools, artistically or analytically, while moving their bodies or sitting still, with visuals or auditorily, they can. If they are gregarious and love to socialize, there are social arenas where they'll thrive. For the ones who keep their circles tight, there are nooks and crannies in which they can feel at ease. The design never forces kids to conform to a single image of how a student should learn.

Wellness

Elsewhere, we see how Baaham can promote a healthier experience while students and teachers are at school. Dining areas aren't built as enormous cafeterias with dozens of tables, which can turn them from places to eat lunch into arenas that reinforce unhelpful social hierarchies. Instead, they're divided into smaller, connected rooms that kids don't feel nervous walking into and that give students the freedom to find their own cozy nooks or groups where they feel comfortable. Within these dining areas, each food item is displayed with nutritional information that nudges people toward healthier choices. Nourishing the students and staff physically allows them to perform better mentally.

Back in the learning environment, students are treated to far more natural light than traditional schools typically provide. Windows are large to avoid an overreliance on artificial lighting, and they are positioned such that students can give their eyes a break by looking out to faraway views of nature. When that's not possible, the spaces are designed with skylights that bathe the interior with warm sunlight and courtyards and gardens that people can enjoy and rooms can look onto. The windows in these rooms are smart enough to recognize when there is a buildup of carbon dioxide, which makes students drowsy, and open automatically in good weather. The learning environment within Baaham schools is always designed to keep students' minds and bodies working well.

Overall, from outside to in, large to small, Baaham schools are built around people's needs. At every moment, the biological preferences and rhythms of the occupants are considered, and spaces are designed to accommodate how students learn best, how teachers teach best, and how administrators lead best with an uncanny ability to adapt and grow right alongside the school.

Imagine if our children could go to a school like this. How much happier might they be? What would it feel like to drop them off at school and see the light in their eyes from the excitement of knowing a great day lies ahead? Every child deserves this experience, and we can give it to them.

Instead of feeling like a number, students can feel like valued members of their communities. Instead of feeling doubtful or afraid, they can feel confident, curious, and able to take risks. And instead of holding them back, their learning environments can push them forward.

Our children deserve this gift. As a society, it may be the greatest one we can give.

15

DESIGN FOR BETTER HEALTH

Doctors take an oath to do no harm. What if our hospitals upheld the same standard?

HOSPITALS THAT CARE FOR OUR WELL-BEING

Have you ever noticed how much we rely on our physical environments to care for and guide us toward better health? We want homes that promote good habits, workplaces that support our minds and bodies, neighborhoods that allow for social and physical activities, grocery stores that offer tasty and nutritious foods, and medical facilities like hospitals, therapy centers, and clinics that nurture us back to health.

Baaham principles can be applied to all these spaces to generate better health. With Baaham, homeowners, designers, developers, governments, and even people running grocery stores and clinics can make decisions that will be good for people. Health facilities, in particular, play an important role in bringing us and our loved ones back to full health—a responsibility that must include a dignified experience for everyone involved, including the doctors, nurses, and staff who work there.

In this chapter, we'll look specifically at hospitals—which play a crucial role in saving lives and restoring health when things have gone awry—and how they can be designed for better patient experiences. More than avoiding harm, hospitals should actively promote positive outcomes: faster healing and recovery, greater comfort, less stress and confusion. Given the stakes involved, shouldn't these facilities be some of the most peaceful, serene places in our society?

CURRENT REALITY

In 2023, my world turned upside down when a valve in my mom's heart ruptured, triggering a cascade of health crises. I spent over eight hundred hours in the hospital with her, sitting in and observing intensive care units, recovery rooms, nurses' stations, counseling rooms, waiting rooms, staff offices, and many other clinical and support spaces. I saw firsthand how hospitals often fail their patients and staff.

In fact, you feel these effects the moment you walk through the front door. A confusing layout immediately disorients you. The stark, cold lighting and hard surfaces create a feeling of sterility. There's no soothing music to put you at ease, just the beeping of machines and rushing of hospital staff. It always feels like something is wrong, like the worst is about to happen.

This is the great irony of how hospitals are designed. They are where we welcome new life into the world and where we say our final good-byes. And yet at nearly every step of the process from admission to discharge, patients, their families, and hospital staff are subjected to indignities. They are forced to cope with an environment that doesn't meet their needs or create a healthy experience. If doctors and nurses must take an oath to do no harm, why aren't the buildings they work in held to the same standard?

If doctors and nurses must take an oath to do no harm, why aren't the buildings they work in held to the same standard?

It wasn't always this way. In the mid-1800s, hospitals benefited tremendously from a young nurse and social reformer named Florence Nightingale. She pioneered a new kind of hospital that was in touch with nature with large, operable windows that let in light and fresh air and created spaces that calmed patients and sped up recovery times.[1] However, as technologies like X-rays, mechanical ventilation, and elevators advanced into the early 1900s, hospitals became superior to house calls, bringing in patients both rich and poor. Overcrowded and armed with new understandings of germ theory, many hospitals closed their windows and began using antibiotics and disinfectants to contain disease, instead of fresh air and sunlight.

Once well-ventilated places of healing, hospitals quickly evolved into the tightly sealed boxes we have today.[2] In these modern buildings, the design focus falls so heavily on turning over patients quickly to optimize costs while maintaining a completely sterile environment that little attention is paid to how a more humane design could speed up patient healing.

One of the most obvious and unrelenting ways hospitals create a negative experience is the amount of visual and auditory stimuli people must confront. Patients have it the worst. As you lie in your hospital bed, in pain but trying your best to stay calm and relaxed, you are surrounded by a cacophony of beeps, buzzes, alarms, and chatter. Your vital signs monitor beeps in time with your heart rate and blood pressure. A separate monitor tracks the drip of IV fluids and chirps incessantly when those fluids run out. Even when all is calm inside your room, out in the hall an intercom occasionally blares "Code Blue" over and over, sending panicked nurses rushing into a neighboring room. You hear this commotion of feet shuffling, carts rolling, and gurneys squeaking because the walls, doors, and dividers are all woefully thin, leaking noise from all corners of the hospital into the place where you're supposed to be resting.

I saw this a few years ago as I accompanied my mom to her hysterectomy surgery at a prominent hospital in Atlanta. I sat beside her bed in the pre-op room, my body shivering and covered in goose bumps because the temperature of the room was kept so low. The lights were dingy and fluorescent. Worst of all, there weren't any walls—only thin curtains that let us hear doctors and patients talking on both sides of us. It all felt so inhumane, and I could see that my mom—one of the calmest people I know—was not relaxed. If someone like her couldn't relax in a place like this, how could anyone?

But patients aren't the only ones who suffer.

For one, operating rooms—where hearts are cut open, bones are repaired, and our lives sometimes hang in the balance—are notoriously difficult to navigate, cluttered with machines, wires, and equipment. The staff who must maneuver around this clutter, not to mention one another, are forced to perform delicate procedures in a fairly chaotic environment. Poor layouts and overcrowding often lead to what researchers call "flow disruptions"—essentially momentary distractions that break surgical staff's concentration and may lead to lower-quality care for the patient. Research indicates that every surgery includes approximately sixty-six disruptions per hour, more than one each minute, with more than 50 percent of those disruptions directly caused by the room's layout, such as a piece of equipment blocking a surgeon's view of the procedure or poor access to the necessary tools and equipment.[3]

During the eight hundred–plus hours I spent in the hospital following my mom's heart valve rupture, I also learned that hospitals rarely meet basic needs for their visitors. The ER examination room lacked windows to let in sunlight or see outside, and there were no outlets for charging my phone and laptop as I sent emails and negotiated with insurance providers.

Since visitors are spending hours, sometimes even days or weeks, with their loved ones, hospitals need to recognize the comfort of their visitors nearly as much as the comfort of their patients. Both are tired, uncertain, and scared. The last thing visitors want is to be hunting around the emergency room for a place to charge their phones.

The design flaws don't end there. All throughout hospitals are clear oversights as to how the space is set up to handle the flow of traffic. After my mom's surgery a few years ago, we learned she needed to be transferred to a post-op wing on the other side of the hospital. This meant hospital staff had to wheel her gurney across a bumpy skybridge, whose floor had raised metal joints every few feet. As I walked beside her gurney, I could see the pain on her face, each bump of the floor causing terrible discomfort. My heart broke for her. This was such a small design feature, but it had enormous consequences for an elderly woman whose body was fragile from surgery. Why didn't the hospital's designers think about who would be traveling along these joints as they planned the skybridge? Why didn't they think about people like my mom?

At every scale, from the patients' direct experiences in their beds to the flow and operations of the building as a whole, hospitals are begging to be redesigned.

PREPARING FOR A BAAHAM HOSPITAL

Designing a Baaham hospital begins with gaining a fuller understanding of the research on how people feel, react, and heal in different contexts. Through direct observational research and even fMRI studies, in which cognitive neuroscientists conduct brain scans of people in different conditions, we learn the factors that help patients get back to full health faster and more comfortably and how their minds and bodies respond to various stimuli. Then we incorporate those insights into our design process.

At every scale, from the patients' direct experiences in their beds to the flow and operations of the building as a whole, hospitals are begging to be redesigned.

For example, we know from research that patients who recover in rooms that face a blank surface, like a brick wall, require more painkillers and higher dosages to get back to full health than people whose recovery rooms face nature, like a tree-filled courtyard. In addition, people with a blank view tend to have worse moods and greater anxiety throughout their stay, even requiring, on average, an extra day of recovery time.[4] Related studies have found similar benefits when people have greater access to daylight in their recovery rooms compared to those whose rooms rely primarily on electric lighting. In both cases, science suggests that nature offers a healing power, and hospitals should make every effort not to isolate patients from the natural world.

When we comb through the research and data and come upon findings like these, we have an obligation to put them to use. They speak to something universal about the ways our minds and bodies go through the healing process.

Other important process changes we can make with Baaham include conducting workshops with families who have recently left a hospital stint to learn from their experience and what they would change. We can also shadow staff to see firsthand what kinds of interruptions and obstacles make their jobs harder and host workshops with them to empathetically understand their pain points. We can bring administrators from the hospital we're designing on a tour of other hospitals around the world—an expense that is well worth it given the stakes involved—to meet with local clinicians and staff, observe how they move through their environment, and see what's working. And we can draw upon our own experiences in hospitals to make note of how we felt, what we liked, and what needed improvement.

To further improve staff performance, we can conduct a careful analysis of the layout and organization of spaces and of the work processes and gauge how well their physiological and operational needs are considered.

For instance, many medical environments have adopted checklists to nudge staff toward making the right decisions and preventing mistakes. Architecture can be designed to do the same. We can design the physical environment so that it prevents the most common mistakes. If staff repeatedly forgets to stock the supply cabinet in the operating room before a surgery starts—which interrupts the procedure because someone then has to retrieve the supplies—the supply cabinet doors could be removed so that missing supplies would be visible and evident to everyone before the surgery begins.

Lastly, we can build into our design process the prototyping of a life-sized hospital room—inspecting it, using it, gauging the experience it creates—before committing to building one hundred rooms just like it. A prototype hospital room would be mocked up with all the right equipment, lights, features, and nearby conditions like noises and distractions to determine how it will perform in the real world. It can help us answer important questions: *Does noise from the hallway enter the room? How easy is it for staff to maneuver and access supplies? Can patients get from their beds to the bathroom safely?*

By the end of this process, it should be clear what patients and their loved ones need to feel comfortable and heal properly and what the hospital staff needs to perform at the highest level.

A VISION FOR BAAHAM HOSPITALS

Once we've completed the design process, we can start to see what a Baaham hospital may look like.

To begin with, every patient gets a private room because that's known to dramatically reduce the risk of hospital-acquired infections. To enter these patient rooms, everyone must pass through a small anteroom. It has airtight doors and creates a pressurized vestibule, which prevents contaminated air from other parts of the hospital from entering the patient's room.

The patient room itself is oriented to get maximum daylight, which improves mood and psychological well-being, reduces depression, reduces pain and blood pressure, and speeds up recovery. The natural light is paired with the room's tuned lighting, which mimics the sun's brightness and dimness across the day, along with bluer temperatures in the morning that slowly shift to amber wavelengths later in the day—to keep the patient's circadian rhythm aligned. There are also blackout shades that automatically go down at night to optimize the patient's sleep and preserve immune function.[5] If patients need to get up in the middle of the night to use the bathroom, a dim light around the doorframe helps them stay oriented in the dark. This minimizes the risk of dangerous nighttime falls.

The windows are operable, so the patient gets fresh air too. Between the windows is a door to the outside. The patient has direct access to a lush garden since immersion in nature can lower cortisol levels—a measure of stress—and soothe agitated patients.[6] The garden has walking paths, benches to sit with visitors and soak up sun, and mounds of colorful flowers and plants.

It's quiet in the room. The monitors for the patient's heart rate, blood pressure, breathing, IV fluids, and others have been reengineered to work quietly so the patient can rest. Notifications are sent to nurses' devices as well as discreet displays in the hallways. Walls have sound-abating insulation, and doors have seals to prevent noises from the hallway from entering the room while the patient rests. The room has smart sensors that help nurses monitor worrisome behavioral changes and whether the patient is restless so they can be quick to provide the right care. The room's sen sors even detect the subtle movements of the heart and lungs to determine heart rate and respiration.[7] At night, patients can sleep comfortably without being tied to several machines that restrict movement and create noise.

The interior design of a Baaham hospital further reduces the spread of infectious diseases. For instance, toilet seats have lids so droplets of waste don't spread around rooms, and increased ventilation allows in more fresh air to dilute virus particles in the interior air (this is also designed to function quietly so the room stays quiet); ample storage exists for staff supplies and the patient's personal items (so there are fewer objects and surfaces for virus-containing droplets to land on); and sinks and hand disinfectants are located near the points where clinicians will provide care so they're more likely to see them and less likely to transfer bacteria from one patient to another.

And if patients are ever feeling sad or anxious, in addition to spending time in the garden, their rooms have soft sensory objects to improve their mood. By holding, squeezing, or caressing a soft item, the patient can feel calmer and more at ease.[8]

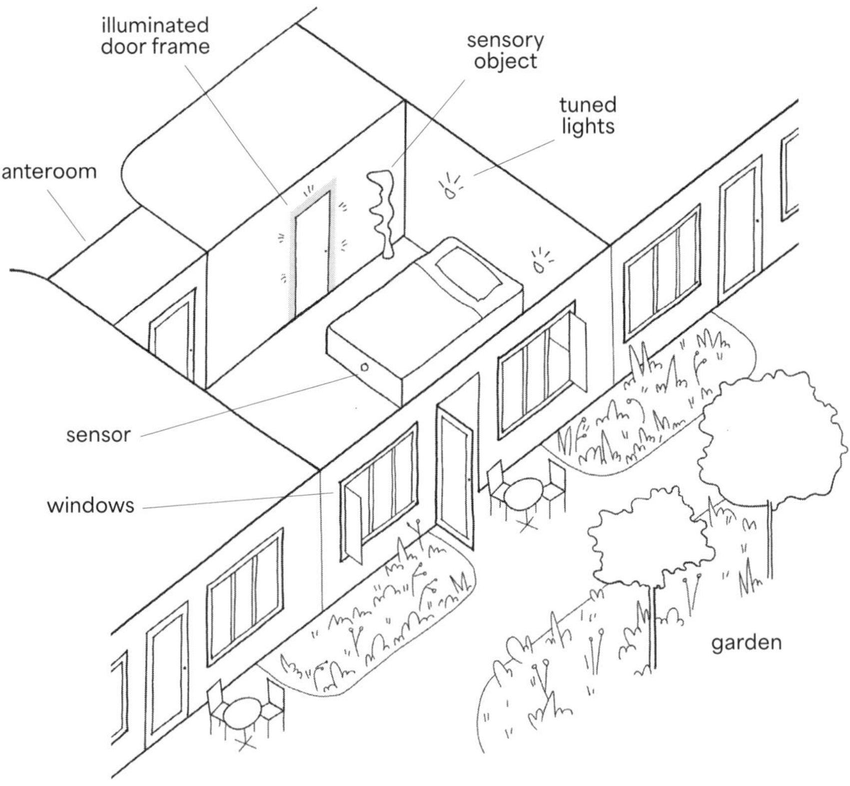

Like the patients' rooms, the ER exam rooms are also quiet. But upon arrival to the emergency room, patients will first be assessed for contagiousness. If deemed a threat to other patients, they'll be taken through separate doors that lead directly to private isolation rooms, where they can't spread viruses to other patients in the waiting area.

Once inside the ER exam rooms, patients won't feel uneasy or embarrassed to share the details of their medical issues because they'll meet with a doctor in a private room, not in between curtains, where others can hear them. Studies have shown this change from curtains to walls often leads to better communication between the patient and the doctor, which leads to better care.[9]

Since coming to the emergency room can be scary and nerve-racking, patients will be kept at ease by being able to choose soft soundscapes to play in the room, making it feel more like a spa. There are no beeps of worry. And because a patient (and worried friend or family member who has accompanied them) could be there for hours, even the ER exam rooms face the internal courtyard and garden. They have large windows for lots of natural light and fresh air.

Staff spaces such as nurses' stations and clinicians' offices are no longer landlocked in the building's core. Instead, they have access to lots of sunlight and to exterior gardens so nurses and doctors have a place to decompress. Staff members are even seen having meetings on the benches in the garden. The offices and stations don't have stark walls but rather elaborate carvings with complex patterns found in nature so workers have something beautiful and positive to look at, emotionally helping them through tough days.

The operating room—where the stakes are arguably the highest—has been redesigned in a few notable ways (based on current technology and protocols) to minimize flow disruptions. Instead of the standard layout, in which the operating table sits in the center of the room, Baaham operating rooms turn the table on its axis and position it diagonally in the room, angling out from the top left corner. The room is rectangular, longer than it is wide, and roughly 570 square feet. In this orientation, the flow of people and supplies in the room is optimized.[10] It also creates a corner at the head of the table where the anesthesiologist can work without interruption and allows nurses to quickly and easily get to the operating table, their nurses' station, and the supply storage at the bottom right of the room—especially when time is of the essence.

Baaham hospitals also recognize that operating rooms can make it difficult for nurses to see vital information. As one nurse described to me, sometimes they're across the room gathering supplies or preparing equipment and, at the same time, need to know what's going on with the patient. By mounting easy-to-read displays around the room that show vital signs, as well as a top-down camera with a prominent high-resolution display, all staff will have the information they need right when they need it. No longer do nurses need to rush over to the table and crowd the patient to get needed information.

To help visitors feel more at ease as their loved ones undergo procedures, waiting rooms on patient floors feel like a cozy den in a home. There visitors can find lamps, sconces, and soft lighting; plush seating; ornate walls with beautiful and comforting patterns; calming paint colors so the stress and discomfort of being in a hospital are reduced; and rich woods on the walls, furniture, and ceilings, as natural material has been shown to steady people's heart rates and blood pressure.[11]

The emotional ergonomics of this space are comforting. There are enough outlets, tables for food and drinks, lockers and cubbies to store personal belongings, and blankets and pillows for family members staying the night. Visitors can also enjoy furniture that's comfortable for long stays, ample natural light, a reasonable temperature, humidity control, and an overall feeling of coziness.

None of this comes at the expense of thinking about the location of the hospital building itself. Baaham hospitals are built on abandoned or underutilized land known as "brownfield" sites so that their presence improves the area, rather than occupying a "greenfield" (virgin) site. The hospital is powered by renewable energy sources, and the building is constructed from materials that are healthy, nontoxic, renewable, and upcycled.

Plus, the building is smart. It has systems that passively and actively collect feedback on how the space is performing against its goals of promoting health, recovery, and support and how it's doing for families, patients, staff, and clinicians. This data is made open so that anyone around the world who plans to build a hospital can design a better one using the insights from this hospital.

+ + +

Baaham hospitals aren't the stuff of fantasy. These changes are possible if we stop putting profit and efficiency over the well-being and comfort of the people who depend on hospitals: patients, visitors, and staff.

In the early 1900s, we began to lose touch with the idea that our physical environments can keep us healthy. But when we take the right design steps, we can transform the kind of care we deliver to people in the most frightening moments of their lives. We can comfort them. We can care for them. We can make their darkest days feel more hopeful. And if they are coming to the end of their time here, we can fill their final moments with dignity and compassion.

Hospitals are wonders of medical science. With Baaham, we have the power to make them wonders of design as well, capable of life-saving and life-giving potential.

16

DESIGN FOR BETTER COMMUNITY

The best public spaces produce unyielding happiness.

NEIGHBORHOODS THAT MAKE SPACE FOR JOY

Whether we live in big cities or small towns, in suburban subdivisions or bustling metropolises, the design of our communities shapes our lives in undeniable ways. It affects our moods, our physical and mental health, our relationships with loved ones and strangers, and how much time we spend doing the things we find important.

Where we live, shop, eat, work, and socialize, and the landscape connecting it all, are what contain our lives. We want our communities to support us, to help us connect with others, and to make us feel like we belong. We want convenient access to services such as doctor's offices and local grocery stores. We want to feel safe wherever we go and to know that people look out for one another. We want the community to be a nurturing and enriching place to raise children. And we want easy access to beautiful and enjoyable outdoor spaces that offer a connection to nature. We might also hope for other things such as minimal noise and traffic congestion and a general sense of cleanliness. I know I want these things wherever I live.

We want our communities to support us, to help us connect with others, and to make us feel like we belong.

Many kinds of communities can be designed with Baaham. In this chapter, we'll focus on a medium-sized community that blends elements of a vibrant city and a quaint village. This isn't to suggest that this is the best type of community. With Baaham, many different types of communities can emerge. This is simply one illustration of how good our communities can be when designed with Baaham.

CURRENT REALITY

On a practical level, our communities are where we live our lives together. But they should also come to *reflect*, through their design and architecture, what we care about. Unfortunately, both outcomes tend to be neglected.

Two major forces are at work. The first is the group of people responsible for building cities for us: the urban planners, developers, government workers, architects, traffic engineers, and others who have been trained to think in ways that may do more harm than good to a community.

Architecture schools reward attention-grabbing designs. So architects-in-training learn to put bold shapes and aesthetics over healthy or humanistic designs. Traffic engineers are taught to design automobile-centric roads. Urban planners and city officials get bombarded with economic concerns over livability. And through their years in business, developers learn that cheap materials and practices, not sustainability, are better for their bottom line.

The second force at work are the objectives that result from misguided priorities. When developers and city officials thirst for money, they abandon good placemaking and simply replicate trending urban features and gimmicky spaces that lure young professionals to move and spend money there. Architects are also guilty of focusing on a narrow objective: creating stellar buildings. We concentrate on how the public will experience our singular building and sometimes forget to consider how people experience that street or neighborhood as a whole. When every building is designed to stand out, our neighborhoods come to feel like a hodgepodge of mismatched objects.

Some of the worst objectives, however, are those enshrined in the laws that dictate where buildings can be constructed and how people can travel around their community. For example, zoning laws often separate different land for different uses—houses here, offices there, stores somewhere else. Our laws also limit density, creating a sprawling environment where our homes are necessarily far away from local offices and stores. And because laws say places must have parking for cars, destinations that we could get to by walking or biking are accessible only by driving because they're separated by massive parking lots. Such an approach to community building does not end well.

Here's what we live with: Most communities in America separate shops, homes, and offices. There's a central business area where city leaders concentrate investments, leaving underdevelopment everywhere else. Retail spaces are clustered into shopping centers, instead of being strategically located near our homes, so we're forced into the choice between making special trips to congested strip malls or big-box stores or shopping exclusively online.

We usually make these trips by driving because our communities don't offer many other options. Few bus or subway routes exist. Bikes aren't given enough space to be safe. And with everything spread apart, we can't walk to the places we want to go. Is it any wonder kids today almost exclusively hang out online and adults stay cooped up at home? We've traded visits to the neighborhood park to staying put in our private yards. Instead of going to the community pool, we build expensive pools in our backyards. Instead of going to the movies, we build elaborate home theater systems in our basements. Everything we used to do communally now happens privately, at home, alone. Poor suburban design breeds social isolation.

We can think of this design failure as building at an inhuman scale. In the suburbs, this happens horizontally—everything is spread too far apart. In cities we do the same thing, only the failure happens vertically. Residents live so high up in towers that they lose connection to the ground, where communal life happens. Both figuratively and literally, we're not grounded. How might this physical distance from one another—from civic life in both cities and suburbs—lead to feelings of disconnection from our fellow humans?

At the same time, our communities don't feel as safe or inclusive as we'd like. Cyclists are regularly hit, the elderly can't get around safely, and women fear walking alone at night because there aren't enough people around to have eyes on the street. For example, a lack of safe spaces where girls can hang out and play without fear of violence or sexual crimes causes their world to shrink. Studies show that the day-to-day movement of a fourteen-year-old girl is only two-fifths the distance of her eleven-year-old self and only one-third the distance of a fourteen-year-old male peer's movement.[1]

Our communities are also unsafe for our health. Because we're forced to drive, we shoulder the responsibility to stay physically active through our finite supply of willpower, versus our environments nudging us toward healthier behaviors by default. The same happens on a social level: Car-centric communities nudge us away from striking up conversations with strangers, instead pitting us as adversaries on the road. The design of our communities even changes how we think about other humans who don't get around the way the design says they should. Have you ever driven through a suburban area and seen someone walking along the side of a local highway and questioned why they're walking? Maybe you assume they're too poor to afford a car, or you make other snap judgments about them. Now picture that person with a different background, in an urban area with defined sidewalks. Suddenly walking is completely normal. In both cases, the person's action is the same. It's only because we as society failed to provide a sidewalk that we have a negative perception of that person.

All of those shortcomings might be easier to tolerate if our communities looked good. But they don't. They're austere and unnatural. Ugly.

Characterless. There's little beauty. Company logos, billboards, and flashing signs make our communities feel like they exist for advertising.

We don't have to live like this. We can design communities well so that we have choice in how we move, how we access important services and green spaces, and whether we enjoy a good quality of living.

Baaham can bring that vision to life.

PREPARING FOR A BAAHAM COMMUNITY

To design a Baaham community, we need an interdisciplinary and inclusive design process. We'll gather many disparate viewpoints to inform how the community should work. In addition to urban planners, architects, civil engineers, and people specializing in infrastructure and landscape, we'll include people who study complex systems, mathematics, robotics, transportation, information technology, and sociology—not to mention the greatest stakeholders of them all: everyday citizens.

To design a Baaham community, we need an interdisciplinary and inclusive design process.

Together, we'll host inclusive workshops where people can voice their concerns, views, and wishes and hear from others. We'll gain perspective and think as a community about the relationship between work and family, how to create suitable public institutions in each neighborhood, and what community members want their days and weeks to look like.

In this codesign process, we'll identify the important criteria for this Baaham community, such as improved health, connection to nature, a sense of belonging, convenience, and comfort. This exercise, a version of the lightbulb exercise we saw in *Embrace Details*, will illuminate the various criteria that will make the design successful. For instance, we know that when senior citizens walk just fifteen minutes per day, their risk of premature death drops by roughly 22 percent.[2] We can use such insights to design neighborhoods for healthier living, while keeping in mind the other goals of the community so they can all be realized together.

With these goals in front of us, we can zoom out to see how the pieces of a community—streets, blocks, buildings, plazas, parks, infrastructure—might fit together. Everyone is reminded that every brick we lay affects people's quality of life, so the team proceeds with humility, knowing it has the opportunity to push this part of society one step closer to the kind of place we want to live in. For this reason, no one tries to make his or her building, park, or bridge an egotistic sculpture; every development and planning decision is recognized as part of a larger ensemble—the community—that guides how people live.

While building, the community's long-term interests are kept in mind, meaning new development solutions are attuned to local climate and geography. This local approach, which includes sourcing nearby materials, leads to an environment that feels unique and charming.

Lastly, we'll weave experimentation into our design process. We'll test solutions on a small scale—say, turning a parking lot into a pop-up park—before deciding whether it makes sense to deploy fuller versions across the entire community. Through trial and error, we'll uncover the solutions that make this Baaham community the best it can be.

A VISION FOR BAAHAM COMMUNITIES

When communities are designed with Baaham principles, people enjoy living there.

People are physically and mentally healthier because they're more active and closer to nature. Their daily lives are less of a grind and more convenient because the services and stores they need are close by. They feel safer because the neighborhood can more easily keep watch. They have more fulfilling relationships with their friends, neighbors, coworkers, and even strangers they meet. Living here makes them feel like they're part of a supportive group.

When we bring community members into the design process, we'll likely find that they care most about health, nature, belonging, convenience, and comfort. The design of their environment reflects those concerns. For example, there's a dense transportation network that allows people to travel in many ways based on their personal mobility and preference: They can walk along active streets, cycle on generous bike lanes, hop on buses, ride reliable subways, or drive if desired.

While no single transit system can take people everywhere, in a Baaham community, residents find commuting easy because at every stop, different transit lines intersect. People can get off the subway and grab a bike or hop on a streetcar toward their destination. With such an interconnected system, residents can quickly get from their homes to workplaces, grocery stores and other shops, schools, health services, and hot spots for leisure and recreation. And because they're biking and walking more, which are affordable and equitable ways of getting around for everyone, people are healthier.[3]

One reason everyone here is happier, healthier, and more comfortable than in other communities is that the streets were designed for them to enjoy instead of being designed to move cars. Streets are a *destination.* People are out and about, walking on wide, tree-lined sidewalks, passing by shops and businesses.

What makes these streets so desirable? The secret lies with the ground floors.

A Baaham community has mixed uses. So while there may be housing and offices above, the ground floors can be retail. That means the edge, where buildings meet sidewalks, is lively. Restaurants and cafés spill onto the sidewalk with outdoor tables. Bookstores pull shelves onto the sidewalk, and people stop to flip through books. The edge is porous, overflowing with people moving in and out. Pedestrians can walk close to the road because cars aren't whizzing past dangerously.

If you walk along this exciting edge, eventually you will reach a piazza, an open square encircled by buildings that often serves as the heart of public life. You'll see people entering the square from all sides, fed by the community's main streets. Like outdoor rooms, the various piazzas around the community are cozy. Some people are walking across them, while others stop to hang out around the perimeter. They're sitting on benches facing the square, their backs protected against the buildings so they can people-watch as they please.

Leafy trees hover over portions of the piazza like natural awnings and offer shade to the people below as they chat with friends and watch their kids play. The trees keep the temperature cool, provide some privacy for personal conversations, and clean the air.

When people are done strolling and need to get somewhere quickly, the streets help them. They're laid out in a square grid with occasional diagonals, which give people the fastest way to walk somewhere. Beyond the community's widest streets, which are the main destinations and are active with people getting around, are narrower streets—paths, essentially—that feel less like destinations and more like stepping into a serene neighborhood. It's quiet here. Buildings are short; people are biking and walking; kids are running and playing all over. Many people in this Baaham community live off these paths.

With fewer cars buzzing around, the community needs less space for parking.[4] So it has built more housing for people. For this community, Baaham has helped alleviate the chronic housing shortage felt in so many cities. Every neighborhood in the community has a balance of housing options for families, couples, individuals, and group households. While the community has what I would call "gentle density"—buildings on small streets that are two to three stories and central streets with buildings of four to six stories—it feels extremely livable. In fact, the density enhances livability. With people living closer together, more space is available to be used as parks, green spaces, walking paths, and other pleasing natural environments for people to enjoy.[5]

Because there are housing options on all streets, people can live where they want. Some have chosen to live on a quiet, secluded street. They prefer privacy. Others are living above shops and restaurants because they want to be able to go downstairs and be among lively neighborhood amenities. They want contact.

On the quieter streets, some people are living in side-by-side homes that share walls. Normally these "row houses" are dark inside because their long walls touch neighboring units, and only the short ends have windows bringing in light. Here, these houses are turned ninety degrees so neighbors touch on short walls, and the long walls face the street and backyard. The rotation and undulating walls give residents more sunlight and is more visually interesting from the street. Along the street are stoops in front of homes. People hang out here, striking up conversations with neighbors and passersby. This leads to more friendliness and trust in the community.[6]

The people living above the ground floor shops are also thriving. Some of them live in three- to four-story housing hills, meaning the apartments are stacked in a staggered pattern on a gentle slope. This terraced effect brings light into homes and onto the streets below. And because the hill's

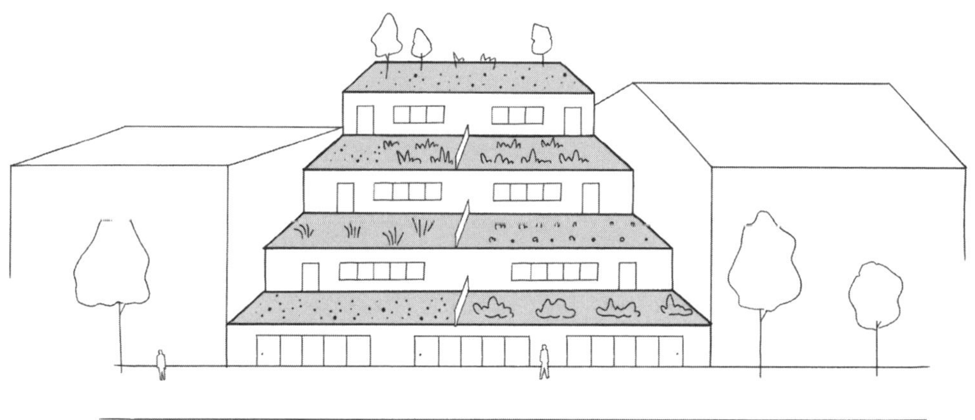

slope faces south and gets sun most of the day, each resident has a private garden. This housing hill efficiently bring residents together with ample access to nature while beautifying the communal space.

But no matter where they live in the neighborhood, people have convenient access to shops and services. For those living on the lively streets, the shops are downstairs. Meanwhile, people on the quieter backstreets can walk around the corner to a main street and access the shops and services. And because housing and shops are mixed on the same blocks, with only a slight turn of the head, you can see a pharmacist, grocery store, gym, bank, post office, coffee shop, and several restaurants of all different cuisines. As people walk to the corners of the streets, they find some of the most vibrant storefronts like Parisian-style cafés and restaurants that have occupied the entire corner with outdoor seating. There's an energy at these active corners.

The web of businesses spread across the city is more than restaurants and clothing stores. Offices are dispersed too. Instead of being in a central business area, workplaces exist in every neighborhood. Most people can walk, bike, or take a streetcar to work. Within a few minutes of their homes are dozens of workplaces, and within fifteen to twenty minutes are hundreds of opportunities.[7]

In this Baaham community, work doesn't happen separate from family life—all of it happens simultaneously. With home and work so close, workers meet their families for lunch, partners stop by the office to drop off something, and workers run home if they need something. Walking through a piazza, you see this firsthand. Around lunchtime, a young man meets up with his wife and children to share a meal outside. Nearby, a woman in business attire hops on a bike and takes off down a street, perhaps headed for home. In the full light of day, you notice that most people seem to be smiling. They don't seem to be coping or struggling with their day. They seem to be savoring it.

During these lunch breaks or on leisurely days, people have many places for playing, socializing, and gathering. Public amenities can be found every few blocks. You see active parks, buzzing promenades, and social pavilions that are semi-enclosed, with roofs and columns but no walls, to let air and light flow in while people hang out.

You sit to watch a few groups of people. Some groups, like picnickers in the park, seem ready to linger for hours. Others, like the pairs of people seated on benches engrossed in conversations, may be on their lunch breaks. A combination of trees, roof trellises, and balcony overhangs creates just the right amount of sunlight and shade for these interactions. Every so often, a food vendor has set up a cart or small truck for people to enjoy. There are plenty of free and clean public restrooms, hydration points that let people fill up on clean drinking water, and communal tables where people can sit and chat. There's even a two-story urban lighthouse: a small tower in the piazza that people ascend to gain an elevated vantage point over the area. And with water features like ponds and fountains, which complement the greenery surrounding the amenities, the cityscape never feels inhospitable. The people spending time here seem to enjoy a public kind of privacy—fully immersed within a civic realm but comfortably protected in their own personal spaces.

If we take a spot on a public lawn, we have a long sight line of the community, including a glimpse of one of the many local playgrounds. Around the playground, parents are mostly enjoying the company of other parents. They aren't hovering over their children because they know the playground is in full view of the rest of the public space, and the community has been designed to promote safety through visibility and personal connection. Kids are climbing rock walls, traversing obstacle trails, leaping across tree stumps, and building their strength, flexibility, and confidence in the process.

As the sun sets, the playground remains friendly to children, especially young girls. As the lights kick on, the playground remains a well-lit space to play safely. The playground is also surrounded by buildings—housing, offices, shops—so eyes are on it all day and evening. To help girls feel even more welcome, the playground is designed more around general play than specific sports, which tend to attract boys and deter girls. It also has designated "girls-only" windows at specific times of day, which can make the playground feel less threatening and encourage girls to participate.

Adults play as well. Across the Baaham community are a network of indoor and outdoor wellness centers for keeping up with physical and mental health. They're nestled within the fabric of daily life, so they're easy to get to, and they facilitate activities like swimming, dancing, sports, yoga, meditation, and more.

For adults and kids, spaces like these are "third places"—meaning a place between home and work or school, where people integrate with their communities. Other third places include gaming halls, technology centers, outdoor gyms, and cultural spaces. Together, these create a magnetic pull toward civic life, drawing people out of their homes and into the energy and vibrancy of a community where they can feel a sense of belonging.

A community like this, where our daily necessities of education, employment, housing, health care, and recreation are available within a fifteen-minute walk or bike ride, is possible.

We can build Baaham communities that facilitate people's health and happiness and encourage people to come together in the spirit of one. We can embrace a model of development that doesn't jeopardize the future of our planet or children. A Baaham community is the largest living embodiment of the power of physical space to improve our lives.

So let's begin the work of building a more Baaham world.

PART 4

LET'S GET TO WORK

Baaham means two things working together in tandem, influencing each other. Through its core principles, each of us can become attuned to this relationship in the spaces we inhabit and can begin to make the necessary changes so that our health and well-being are supported. In this final section, you'll hear one more powerful story of how a Baaham space can transform a life, and I hope you'll feel inspired to make the same kind of impact as you venture back into the world.

17

THE WORLD THAT AWAITS US

Through purposeful design, we can create the lives we want most.

ONE SPACE CAN CHANGE YOUR LIFE

When I was in elementary school, the poor design of a bathroom led to an entire day of discomfort and many days of embarrassment. When I was in high school, the failure to consider noise in our classrooms made the testing environment so loud I could hardly concentrate, and my poor score proved it. I feared for my chances at getting into a good college and achieving my goals in life.

It wasn't until I was twenty-six years old and had arrived at Harvard's Graduate School of Design that I was in a learning environment that inspired me, supported my creativity, and helped me learn.

Built in 1972, Gund Hall, the school's main building, isn't what you'd necessarily call "pretty." Its concrete exterior is a plain gray, and the interiors may seem like a chaotic mess at first glance. But the building was so thoughtfully designed that it just seems to understand human nature and what students need to come together and learn from one another. I've found myself incorporating elements of its design when I've designed learning spaces for students.

Along with serving as a common circulation area, the ground floor functions as a gallery for completed projects. Every day, from the moment you walk in, you can see what your peers who are studying different disciplines have been dreaming up and become inspired by their ideas.

And as inspiring as this is, the real magic happens above.

Floors two through five are known collectively as "the trays." They are staggered studios that slant back in a terrace pattern. What is incredible about these studios is that as you walk to the café or the bathroom or a seminar class, you pass individual desks. These desks not only give each student a home base to spread out and do work, make a mess, leave it, and continue the creative flow the next day, but they also serve as mini galleries—because when you walk past someone's work, something interesting might catch your eye. You might stop and chat about the project, and you might even learn a new skill from the person. For example, even though I was studying urban design, every day I was exposed to work from landscape architects, urban planners, and design technologists since we all shared the space.

These kinds of interactions happened all the time at Gund Hall. There was an energy in the building. It felt like we were all one, like ants hustling around a colony or bees busy in their hive. Even at night, you could feel this energy. During the day, at least three hundred people would be using the space. At night, there might be just a handful of night owls still toiling away at their projects. But because of the building's layout, you still sensed their presence. Seeing them working with such dedication and passion pushed you. The enthusiasm and energy that radiated from others, across the open space, was motivating.

Occasionally, students presented their projects to their classes. Here, the open floor plan served a nice purpose (instead of just creating more noise, as is the case in many modern offices). From different floors, you could see the person presenting. You could hear the feedback and learn what other students were learning, even if you weren't in their class.

The space itself is perfectly set up for makers and doers. It isn't a conventional school building. You can tack drawings and posters to the walls. The floors feel industrial, so there is no fear of spilling or breaking anything. Nothing feels precious. This gave us all a sense of creative freedom to use the space however we wanted, to build what needed building.

Gund Hall taught me what a great learning space can look like. It doesn't need to look modern or sleek or have the school's colors everywhere. It doesn't need dozens of identical classrooms. I saw how valuable it is to have different spaces in which to learn and work: fabrication labs, seminar halls, presentation pits, design studios, cafés and common spaces, pinup corners, and galleries for exhibits. Learning spaces can be designed to create connections between students and to accommodate their different learning styles. And learning spaces can be designed so students aren't afraid to try something new and make a mess. When students feel like the space is built for them to learn, they feel a sense of agency to use it how they please, not how they think they're supposed to. That's how true learning happens, and I have Gund Hall to thank for letting me experience it firsthand.

Looking back, I dare say that one building changed my life.

Who knows what kind of architect I would have become if not for all those transformative experiences in grad school, if I hadn't had a great space to inspire me every day as I met incredible peers coming up with brilliant solutions for society's problems?

The design of the building expanded my world. I didn't have to work to expose myself to new ideas; the building did that for me. Just by going there to work every day, I learned how fulfilling life can be when you're in a great space that pushes you toward your dreams. It's something I'm paying forward through my current projects. As of this writing, I've taken what I learned at Gund Hall about creating a supportive place for learning and used it to design schools and learning centers for twenty thousand children.

This is how great spaces change our lives: not always in an instant, but in thousands of inspirational moments that push us to reach our potential.

DESIGNING THE WORLD WE WANT

I hope that as you've read this book, you've seen how Baaham can give us the world we want to live in. If we're able to change our thinking and refocus on why we build before considering what or how to build, we can achieve great things. We can have exactly the kinds of lives we want most.

This is how great spaces change our lives: not always in an instant, but in thousands of inspirational moments that push us to reach our potential.

Instead of debating between visual styles, let's recognize that every shape, color, material, and ornament we choose has a function that influences experience. How something looks affects how it works, which means it affects how we think, feel, and behave. And while we try to optimize for how we can build cheaper and faster to bring architecture to more people, let's remember that if we lose sight of why we're designing, we may end up with something we don't really need. Our optimization won't matter if we've optimized for the wrong result.

Baaham encourages us to rethink what it means for architecture to succeed or fail. A building's tragic collapse isn't the first sign that it has failed. By Baaham standards, architecture fails when it fails to live up to the needs of the people using a space—if it's overly stressful or damaging to our quality of life or if it "falls down on the job."[1]

You can apply the wisdom of Baaham everywhere because our built environments are affecting us at every scale.

The design of urban environments affects our ability to get around, maintain physical health, accomplish our daily tasks, and feel a sense of belonging. Whether we're forced to cope with standstill automobile traffic or free to cruise along open bike paths; whether we're stressed in our jobs and personal lives or feel light and joyful; and whether we're wasting time getting around or enjoying the company of our families—it all depends on the quality of design at the urban scale.

Individual buildings affect our thoughts, feelings, moods, and physical performance too. Are we getting enough natural light, fresh air, and distant views? Or do our eyes hurt, and are we lethargic because we lack these elements? Do our bedrooms lack the proper vents to regulate air pressure? Do we wake up with congested sinuses, feeling dried out because the vents are blocked or missing? Every building we use exerts forces on us at every moment, whether we realize it or not.

How these buildings are laid out—their interior designs—adds a third layer to our experience. Are the paint colors, noise levels, and visual details on the walls distracting and chaotic, or are they calming? If we want to feel more energized, do they support alertness? When it comes to getting things done, do we have adequate space allotted for what we need? The placement of interior elements—the layout of rooms, furnishings, and technology—can dictate how we interact with others, how we focus and work, and how we feel.

Even individual pieces of furniture play a role in how well we perform and how we feel. A desk made from the wrong material may feel uncomfortably cold, and a couch whose seat is too deep can leave us with backaches. These aren't mild inconveniences. They are predictable aggravations that keep us from staying productive, in good health, and fully present with others.

All of these scales of architecture matter. They all, in their own ways, affect the quality and character of our lives. We must remember that problems in architecture aren't just architects' problems. They're everyone's problems because we all live inside architecture.

Design affects us all.

A VISION FOR A BAAHAM WORLD

I'm optimistic for the future we can create with Baaham. I envision a world that helps people experience more happiness, more convenience, and more enjoyable lives. People live in homes that support great sleep, nutritious diets, loving relationships, safety and security, and feelings of joy and contentment. Communities are laid out in ways that nurture physical and mental health. They create moments of social connection because places are safe, vibrant, and beloved.

We must remember that problems in architecture aren't just architects' problems. They're everyone's problems because we all live inside architecture. Design affects us all.

In a Baaham world, people trust one another and their institutions. They trust their schools to educate their children. They trust their hospitals to be humane places of healing. They trust their grocery stores to encourage healthy eating habits. They trust their local government to keep their best interests in mind. A world built with Baaham is one where we can flourish equally, in every space we occupy.

Just reading this book means you care about your built environment. You acknowledge its influence. Many people never come to this realization, so they stay victims to their surrounding world. Not you. You now have tools to start changing your surroundings for the better.

If you're an architect, engineer, or designer, try to incorporate a teaching from Baaham into your next project. If you work in government, think about how Baaham can improve your process to create better places for the citizens under your care. If you work in real estate development, examine what your architects and designers are providing and whether it lives up to a Baaham standard. If you're a hobbyist or homeowner, review the principles of Baaham, and pick a couple to apply to your next DIY project. If you're hiring architects or designers, evaluate how deeply they think about the process and whether they're creating a place that produces a great result—not just visually, but socially, environmentally, and for your needs.

As I said at the beginning of this book, I'm on a journey to change how we think about and design our world, and I need your help. If you've enjoyed this book and learned anything from it, please share it with a friend. Tell a colleague who likes learning new and helpful things. And if you find yourself with a project where Baaham can help, remember to keep this book handy as a reference. Revisit the principles to remind yourself how to approach the process. This will get you the best results.

If you're particularly moved by what you've read, I invite you to take what you've learned and start demanding better. We all need to insist on more Baaham spaces from this point forward; otherwise we'll see a continuation of business as usual. Parents, demand better schools. Employees, demand better workspaces. Taxpayers, demand better communities and spaces for public life. We must not only think differently but act differently too. One space at a time, we must insist on architecture that works.

While we do this important work, we can begin crafting more Baaham places wherever we go. At home, you can look at each room with fresh eyes to evaluate how well the spaces serve your needs. Is there a gap between how you'd like to feel in your space and how it functions? The changes don't have to be big. Ask yourself, *What better experiences can I create with small tweaks to the room's layout, lighting, furniture, colors, and textures?* Even in public places, where we don't tend to have as much agency, Baaham empowers us to notice how a grocery store's layout or the waiting room at a doctor's office may be influencing how we feel and behave. We each hold the power to move through life with architectural awareness, and the more you practice Baaham, the more you'll see its benefits throughout your day.

I've spent my entire life developing and practicing Baaham—from those early days tinkering and building in the back of my parents' dry-cleaning business to running my own studio that uses design to uplift individuals and entire communities through better architecture. The power to create beautiful places lies inside each of us. You already have the power instinctually. With Baaham you can create a world of true beauty. This is the highest achievement of our designed spaces. When we find a building to be beautiful, we're attracted to the way of life the structure promotes. That's how we'll know we've designed the right environment for ourselves: when it all feels beautiful.

A FINAL NOTE

Dear Reader,

Whether this book is your introduction to design or the next step in an ongoing education, I want to thank you. You made a choice to learn more about how our spaces make us who we are.

Design is not about minimalism or maximalism or farmhouse chic or other styles. It's about figuring out how to make life better, and that's what Baaham helps you do. While not all our troubles with health, relationships, and fulfillment are due to our physical environment, every day I notice ways that our spaces can be redesigned.

I don't mean the world is ugly. Rather, our built environment isn't delivering on its potential to support our happiness and well-being. And once you realize just how much our environment shapes us, dreaming of better designs is only natural.

Now we're at an inflection point. We can continue building a suboptimal world, or we can think about how we want to live and build the world that way. So here's what I'd like you to do: With the book still in your hand, pause. Stare off into space, and ask yourself, *Where in my life can I apply Baaham*?

I cannot wait to see the world you design.

Danish

ACKNOWLEDGMENTS

In writing this book, I have disturbed, consulted, and corresponded with a great variety of people, yet I have never once met anything but patience and care. I cannot thank everybody by name, but I would like to record my great debts of gratitude to the following: Alykhan Mohammad, Anjali Joseph, Anum Shah, Ari Hock, Dan Coleman, Emi Day, Ethan Clatterbaugh, Hassan Karimi, Hristiyan Petrov, Jenny Datoo, Joanna Gee, Julie Mosow, Mariana Figueiro, Mary Kollia, Michael Caton, Michael Schein, Nafisa Dhanani Jiwani, Naïma Alibay, Nikita Mahajan, Paul Makovsky, Saad Rajan, Sarosh Nandwani, and Sehreen Noor Ali.

Among them are two friends who over the years slowly opened my eyes to so many ideas such that I am transformed every time I speak with them: Errol King and Kiran Reddy.

I must also acknowledge those whose research and writing has been influential to my understanding of design: Alain de Botton, Bjarke Ingels, Christopher Alexander, Emily Anthes, Jane Jacobs, Michael Hooper, Nikos Salingaros, Stewart Brand, Thomas Heatherwick, and William Whyte. Their insights and spirit are suffused throughout this book.

I also had the pleasure of working with a team of talented professionals who skillfully guided us to publication: Bonnie Honeycutt, Danielle Peterson, Jennifer Garbowski, Michael Aulisio, and Rachel Thompson.

Three people, finally, have my deepest gratitude. First my collaborator, Chris Weller, who pushed me to share my ideas in a book and saw it through with me. Without his day-to-day interest and dedication, I doubt I could have written this book. And finally, to the two individuals who provide incomparable love and support, to whom I owe more than I can say: Noorin Bhanji and Shehnaz Kurani.

NOTES

Chapter 1: A World Sick with Bad Design

1. Alessandra Terra Vasconcelos Rabelo et al., "Effect of Classroom Acoustics on the Speech Intelligibility of Students," *CoDAS* 26, no. 5 (2014): 360–66, https://doi.org/10.1590/2317-1782/20142014026.
2. Lady Catherine Cantor Cutiva and Alex Burdorf, "Effects of Noise and Acoustics in Schools on Vocal Health in Teachers," *Noise and Health* 17, no. 74 (2015): 17, https://doi.org/10.4103/1463-1741.149569.
3. N. Wessolowski et al., "The Effect of Variable Light on the Fidgetiness and Social Behavior of Pupils in School," *Journal of Environmental Psychology*, 39 (2014): 101–08, https://doi.org/10.1016/j.jenvp.2014.05.001.
4. Roger S. Ulrich, "View Through a Window May Influence Recovery from Surgery," *Science* 224, no. 4647 (1984): 420–21, https://doi.org/10.1126/science.6143402.
5. Sandra India-Aldana et al., "Long-Term Exposure to Walkable Residential Neighborhoods and Risk of Obesity-Related Cancer in the New York University Women's Health Study (NYUWHS)," *Environmental Health Perspectives* 131, no. 10 (2023), https://doi.org/10.1289/ehp11538.
6. Louis-Philippe Beland and Daniel A. Brent, "Traffic and Crime," *Journal of Public Economics* 160 (April 2018): 96–116, https://doi.org/10.1016/j.jpubeco.2018.03.002.
7. Christopher Alexander, *The Timeless Way of Building* (Oxford University Press, 1979), 106.
8. Mihaly Csikszentmihalyi, *Flow: The Psychology of Optimal Experience* (HarperCollins, 1990), 8.

Chapter 2: To Be Human Is to Architect

1. Matthew Walker PhD, *Why We Sleep: Unlocking the Power of Sleep and Dreams* (Scribner, 2018).

Chapter 3: The Machine of Bad Design

1. Hassan Fathy, *Natural Energy and Vernacular Architecture: Principles and Examples with Reference to Hot Arid Climates* (University of Chicago Press, 1986).
2. C. Thomas Mitchell, *Redefining Designing: From Form to Experience* (Wiley, 1992).

Chapter 6: Solve Important Problems

1. Sheldon Cohen, David C. Glass, and Jerome E. Singer, "Apartment Noise, Auditory Discrimination, and Reading Ability in Children," *Journal of Experimental Social Psychology* 9, no. 5 (1973): 407–22, https://doi.org/10.1016/s0022-1031(73)80005-8.
2. "Cities Alive: Towards a Walking World," ARUP, 2020, https://www.arup.com/en-us/insights/cities-alive-towards-a-walking-world/.
3. Stewart Brand, *How Buildings Learn: What Happens After They're Built* (Viking Adult, 1994), 137; Lim Jee Yuan, *The Malay House: Rediscovering Malaysia's Indigenous Shelter System* (Pulau Pinang: Institut Masyarakat, 1987).

4. Sim, David. Soft City: *Building Density for Everyday Life*. Washington, DC: Island Press, 2019.

Chapter 7: Design for Change

1. Commons Sitting of 28 October 1943 Series 5 Vol. 393, HOUSE OF COMMONS REBUILDING, cc403–73, https://api.parliament.uk/historic-hansard/commons/1943/oct/28/house-of-commons-rebuilding.
2. "Winston Churchill the Architect?" JEMA, March 6, 2015, https://jemastl.com/2015-2-16-was-winston-churchill-an-architect/.
3. Lorraine E. Maxwell and Suzanne L. Schechtman, "The Role of Objective and Perceived School Building Quality in Student Academic Outcomes and Self-Perception," *Children, Youth and Environments* 22, no. 1 (2012): 23, https://doi.org/10.7721/chilyoutenvi.22.1.0023.
4. Anna V. Fisher, Karrie E. Godwin, and Howard Seltman, "Visual Environment, Attention Allocation, and Learning in Young Children: When Too Much of a Good Thing May Be Bad," *Psychological Science* 25, no. 7 (2014): 1362–70, https://doi.org/10.1177/0956797614533801.
5. Pedro F.S. Rodrigues and Josefa N.S. Pandeirada, "When Visual Stimulation of the Surrounding Environment Affects Children's Cognitive Performance," *Journal of Experimental Child Psychology* 176 (December 1, 2018): 140–49, https://doi.org/10.1016/j.jecp.2018.07.014.
6. David Kestenbaum, host, *Planet Money*, podcast, episode 555, "Why Is the Milk in the Back of the Store?," NPR, September 21, 2016, https://www.npr.org/transcripts/494927147.
7. Stewart Brand, *How Buildings Learn: What Happens After They're Built* (Viking Adult, 1994), 26.
8. Walter Isaacson, *Steve Jobs* (Simon & Schuster, 2011).
9. Joan Meyers-Levy and Rui (Juliet) Zhu, "The Influence of Ceiling Height: The Effect of Priming on the Type of Processing That People Use," *Journal of Consumer Research, Inc.*, 34 (2007), https://assets.csom.umn.edu/assets/71190.pdf.
10. Tisha Lewis Ellison, "Normalizing Black Students/Youth and Their Families' Digital and STEAM Literacies," *The Reading Teacher* 76, no. 5 (2023): 594–600, https://doi.org/10.1002/trtr.2182.
11. Brand, *How Buildings Learn*.
12. The idea of scenario planning was inspired by Stewart Brand. For an extended explanation and further examples, see *How Buildings Learn*, 178–85.
13. Brand, *How Buildings Learn*.
14. John Ruskin, *The Seven Lamps of Architecture* (Project Gutenberg, 2011), https://www.gutenberg.org/files/35898/35898-h/35898-h.htm.

Chapter 8: Follow Nature

1. Milena Damulewicz et al., "Communication Among Photoreceptors and the Central Clock Affects Sleep Profile," *Frontiers in Physiology* 11 (August 10, 2020), https://doi.org/10.3389/fphys.2020.00993.
2. Sato Honma et al., "Suprachiasmatic Nucleus: Cellular Clocks and Networks," *Progress in Brain Research* 199 (2012): 129–41, https://doi.org/10.1016/b978-0-444-59427-3.00029-0.
3. Anjali Joseph, "Impact of Light on Outcomes in Healthcare Settings," Building Research

Information Knowledgebase, January 1, 2006, https://www.brikbase.org/content/impact-light-outcomes-healthcare-settings.

4. “Carbon Dioxide Levels Chart,” CO2 Meter, February 3, 2025, https://www.co2meter.com/blogs/news/carbon-dioxide-indoor-levels-chart.
5. Joseph G. Allen et al., “Associations of Cognitive Function Scores with Carbon Dioxide, Ventilation, and Volatile Organic Compound Exposures in Office Workers: A Controlled Exposure Study of Green and Conventional Office Environments,” *Environmental Health Perspectives* 124, no. 6 (2015): 805–12, https://doi.org/10.1289/ehp.1510037.
6. “Asthma | Healthy Schools | CDC,” n.d., https://www.cdc.gov/healthyschools/asthma/index.htm.
7. Joy Hsu et al., “Asthma-Related School Absenteeism, Morbidity, and Modifiable Factors,” *American Journal of Preventive Medicine* 51, no. 1 (2016): 23–32, https://doi.org/10.1016/j.amepre.2015.12.012.
8. Maria Klatte et al., “Effects of Aircraft Noise on Reading and Quality of Life in Primary School Children in Germany: Results from the NORAH Study,” *Environment and Behavior* 49, no. 4 (2016): 390–424, https://doi.org/10.1177/0013916516642580.
9. Mark Schneider, “Do School Facilities Affect Academic Outcomes?” ERIC, November 2002, https://eric.ed.gov/?id=ED470979.
10. Ilene J. Busch-Vishniac et al., “Noise Levels in Johns Hopkins Hospital,” *Journal of the Acoustical Society of America* 118, no. 6 (2005): 3629–45, https://doi.org/10.1121/1.2118327.
11. Julie L. Darbyshire and J. Duncan Young, “An Investigation of Sound Levels on Intensive Care Units with Reference to the WHO Guidelines,” *Critical Care* 17, R187 (2013): n.p., https://doi.org/10.1186/cc12870.
12. David Barlas et al., “Comparison of the Auditory and Visual Privacy of Emergency Department Treatment Areas with Curtains Versus Those with Solid Walls,” *Annals of Emergency Medicine* 38, no. 2 (2001): 135–39, https://doi.org/10.1067/mem.2001.115441.
13. Weijing Luo et al., “Residential Open Space and the Perception of Health Benefits: How Much Is the Public Willing to Pay?” *Journal of Environmental Management* 316 (August 15, 2022): 115273, https://doi.org/10.1016/j.jenvman.2022.115273.
14. Jason S. Gaekwad et al., “A Meta-Analysis of Emotional Evidence for the Biophilia Hypothesis and Implications for Biophilic Design,” *Frontiers in Psychology* 13 (May 26, 2022), https://doi.org/10.3389/fpsyg.2022.750245.
15. Rebecca A. Clay, “Green Is Good for You!” *Monitor on Psychology* 32, no. 4 (2001): 40, https://www.apa.org/monitor/apr01/greengood.
16. Dongying Li and William C. Sullivan, “Impact of Views to School Landscapes on Recovery from Stress and Mental Fatigue,” *Landscape and Urban Planning* 148 (April 2016): 149–58, https://doi.org/10.1016/j.landurbplan.2015.12.015.
17. Jim Determan et al., “The Impact of Biophilic Learning Spaces on Student Success,” *Architecture Planning Interiors*, 2019, https://www.terrapinbrightgreen.com/wp-content/uploads/2020/01/The-Impact-of-Biophilic-Learning-Spaces-on-Student-Success-1-15-2020.pdf.
18. Emma Kapp, “Biomimicry in Architectural Design: The Bullitt Center,” *PRISM*, May 30, 2017, https://prismpub.com/biomimicry-in-architectural-design-the-bullitt-center/. “Solar Panels,” Bullitt Center, n.d., https://bullittcenter.org/building/building-features/solar-district-1.

Chapter 9: Embrace Details

1. Stewart Brand, *How Buildings Learn: What Happens After They're Built* (Viking Adult, 1994).
2. Charles Spence, "Unraveling the Mystery of the Rounder, Sweeter Chocolate Bar," *Flavour* 2, no. 1 (2013), https://doi.org/10.1186/2044-7248-2-28.
3. R. S. Fixot, "Evaluation of Research on Effects of Visual Training on Visual Functions," *American Journal of Ophthalmology* 44, no. 2 (1957), 230–36, https://www.sciencedirect.com/science/article/abs/pii/0002939457900120.
4. Nikos A. Salingaros, "Why Monotonous Repetition Is Unsatisfying," *Meandering Through Mathematics* (blog), September 2, 2011, https://meandering-through-mathematics.blogspot.com/2011/09/why-monotonous-repetition-is.html.
5. Preservation Green Lab, "The Greenest Building: Quantifying the Environmental Value of Building Reuse," National Trust for Historic Preservation, 2011, https://living-future.org/wp-content/uploads/2022/05/The_Greenest_Building.pdf.
6. The lightbulb exercise was drawn from the work of architect and theorist Christopher Alexander's book *Notes on the Synthesis of Form* (Harvard University Press, 1964).
7. James C-Y Lai and Noel Amaladoss, "Music in Waiting Rooms: A Literature Review," National Library of Medicine, PubMed Central, December 27, 2021, https://pmc.ncbi.nlm.nih.gov/articles/PMC9072951/.
8. Many of the featured examples for complex repetition were drawn from the work of Professor Nikos Salingaros.

Chapter 10: Build Ecologically

1. "Bringing Embodied Carbon Upfront," World Green Building Council, accessed February 18, 2025, https://worldgbc.org/article/bringing-embodied-carbon-upfront/.
2. The materials pyramid indicating the global warming potential of different construction materials was developed by the Center for Industrialized Architecture (CINARK) at the Royal Danish Academy in Denmark and first published in 2019. https://www.materialepyramiden.dk/.
3. Hassan Fathy, *Natural Energy and Vernacular Architecture: Principles and Examples with Reference to Hot Arid Climates* (University of Chicago Press, 1986).
4. Stewart Brand, *How Buildings Learn: What Happens After They're Built* (Viking Adult, 1994).
5. *Britannica*, "cyclopean masonry," last modified by Amy Tikkanen, accessed February 18, 2025, https://www.britannica.com/technology/cyclopean-masonry.
6. "Livable Building: The David & Lucile Packard Foundation Headquarters," project award submittal, Center for the Built Environment, https://cbe.berkeley.edu/wp-content/uploads/2018/07/PackardFoundation-1.pdf.
7. Maddalena Iovene, Nicholas Boys Smith, and Chanuki Illushka Seresinhe, *Of Streets and Squares: Which Public Places Do People Want to Be in and Why?* (Create Streets, 2019), https://issuu.com/cadoganlondon/docs/of_streets_and_squares_26_march_wit.

Chapter 11: Zoom Out

1. Sunandini Ghosh, et al., "Sedentary Lifestyle with Increased Risk of Obesity in Urban Adult Academic Professionals: An Epidemiological Study in West Bengal, India," *Scientific Reports*, 13, no. 4895 (March 25, 2023), https://doi.org/10.1038/s41598-023-31977-y.
2. Tim Newcomb, "Blue Is Probably Your Favorite Color. Here's Why, According to Science,"

Popular Mechanics, June 6, 2022, https://www.popularmechanics.com/science/a40207932/why-blue-is-probably-your-favorite-color/.

3. Nino Wessolowski et al., "The Effect of Variable Light on the Fidgetiness and Social Behavior of Pupils in School," *Journal of Environmental Psychology* 39 (September 2014): 101–8, https://doi.org/10.1016/j.jenvp.2014.05.001.
4. W. U. Weitbrecht et al., "Effect of light color temperature on concentration and creativity," *Advances in Neurology, Psychiatry* 83, no. 6 (2015): 344–48, https://doi.org/10.1055/s-0035-1553051.
5. As of this writing, those technologies are the most cutting-edge, but you may be reading this at a time when even more sophisticated technology is available.

Chapter 12: Design for Better Living

1. Stewart Brand, *How Buildings Learn: What Happens After They're Built* (Viking Adult, 1994); Suzanne LaBarre, "Truth in Numbers," Metropolis, October 1, 2008, https://metropolismag.com/programs/truth-in-numbers/.
2. Alain de Botton, *The Architecture of Happiness* (Hamish Hamilton, 2006).

Chapter 13: Design for Better Working

1. Peter Dizikes, "Proximity Boosts Collaboration on MIT Campus," MIT News, July 9, 2017, https://news.mit.edu/2017/proximity-boosts-collaboration-mit-campus-0710.
2. W. U. Weitbrecht et al., "Effect of light color temperature on concentration and creativity," *Advances in Neurology, Psychiatry* 83, no. 6 (2015): 344–48, https://doi.org/10.1055/s-0035-1553051.
3. John Alker et al. "Health, Wellbeing and Productivity in Offices." World Green Building Council, 2015, https://worldgbc.org/wp-content/uploads/2022/03/compressed_WorldGBC_Health_Wellbeing__Productivity_Full_Report_Dbl_Med_Res_Feb_2015-1.pdf.
4. Excess office noise has been shown to lower performance by up to 66 percent, and noise in general has been found to be detrimental to our health and is linked to sleep disturbance and hypertension. See Goran Belojević, Evy Öhrström, and Ragnar Rylander, "Effects of Noise on Mental Performance with Regard to Subjective Noise Sensitivity," *International Archives of Occupational and Environmental Health* 64, no. 4 (1992): 293–301, https://doi.org/10.1007/bf00378288. See also Göran B. W. Söderlund et al., "The Effects of Background White Noise on Memory Performance in Inattentive School Children," *Behavioral and Brain Functions* 6, no. 55 (2010): n.p., https://doi.org/10.1186/1744-9081-6-55.
5. A workplace's thermal conditions significantly impact employees' satisfaction levels. Poor thermal comfort has been shown to cause up to a 9 percent drop in productivity. See Joseph G. Allen et al., "Associations of Cognitive Function Scores with Carbon Dioxide, Ventilation, and Volatile Organic Compound Exposures in Office Workers: A Controlled Exposure Study of Green and Conventional Office Environments," *Environmental Health Perspectives* 124, no. 6 (2016): 805–12, https://doi.org/10.1289/ehp.1510037.
6. According to Gallup's "State of the Global Workplace: 2021 Report," 43 percent of global employees reported feeling stressed daily. That figure rose to 57 percent for U.S. and Canadian workers. See https://www.gallup.com/workplace/349484/state-of-the-global-workplace.aspx#ite-350777.
7. In terms of wellness, it's important to recognize that indoor environments can be more polluted than the outdoors. The Environmental Protection Agency (EPA) found that

pollutants can be two to five times higher inside and that concentration of volatile organic compounds (VOCs) are often ten times higher indoors than outdoors. In 2023, the World Health Organization (WHO) found that complications from breathing polluted indoor air were responsible for 3.2 million premature deaths each year. See Regina Montero-Montoya, Rocío López-Vargas, and Omar Arellano-Aguilar, "Volatile Organic Compounds in Air: Sources, Distribution, Exposure and Associated Illnesses in Children," *Annals of Global Health* 84, no. 2 (2018): 225–38, https://doi.org/10.29024/aogh.910. See also "Household Air Pollution," World Health Organization, October 16, 2024, https://www.who.int/news-room/fact-sheets/detail/household-air-pollution-and-health.

8. Christopher Alexander, *A Pattern Language: Towns, Buildings, Construction* (Oxford University Press, 1977).

Chapter 14: Design for Better Learning

1. Joshua Fetcher, "Top Texas Republicans Resist Gun Control and Push for More Armed Teachers and Police at Schools in Wake of Uvalde Shooting," *The Texas Tribune*, May 24, 2022, https://www.texastribune.org/2022/05/24/texas-republicans-uvalde-gun-control/; "Hardening Schools Doesn't Work," *National Education Association*, June 15, 2022, https://www.nea.org/resource-library/hardening-schools-doesnt-work; "School Hardening Can Harm Students' Social, Emotional, and Academic Development," EdTrust, April 6, 2023, https://edtrust.org/press-room/school-hardening-can-harm-students-social-emotional-and-academic-development/; Tim Walker, "School Hardening Not Making Students Feel Safer," *National Education Association*, February 14, 2019, https://www.nea.org/nea-today/all-news-articles/school-hardening-not-making-students-safer-say-experts; Danish Kurani, "I Design Schools. Hardening Them Isn't the Answer to School Shootings," Kurani website, 2022, https://kurani.us/hardening-school-design-bad-solution-uvalde/.

Chapter 15: Design for Better Health

1. Florence Nightingale, Notes on Hospitals, 3rd ed. (Longman, Green, Longman, Roberts, and Green, 1863).
2. C. Robert Horsburgh, "Healing by Design," *The New England Journal of Medicine* 333 (1995): 735–40; Angela Burke, "Towards a New Hospital Architecture: An Exploration of the Relationship Between Hospital Space and Technology" (PhD diss., University of East London, 2014). Zimring and DuBose, "Healthy Health Care Settings," 2056.
3. Anjali Joseph et al., "Minor Flow Disruptions, Traffic-Related Factors and Their Effect on Major Flow Disruptions in the Operating Room," *BMJ Quality and Safety* 28, no. 4 (2018): 276–83, https://doi.org/10.1136/bmjqs-2018–007957.
4. This research primarily took place in the 1980s and was conducted by Roger Ulrich, PhD, who analyzed patient recovery times following gallbladder surgery at Pennsylvania hospitals. See R. S. Ulrich, "View Through a Window May Influence Recovery from Surgery," *Science* 224, no. 4647 (1984): 420–21, https://www.science.org/doi/10.1126/science.6143402.
5. Amira Moustafa, "Chronic Exposure to Continuous Brightness or Darkness Modulates Immune Responses and Ameliorates the Antioxidant Enzyme System in Male Rats," *Frontiers in Veterinary Science* 8, no. 621188 (2021), https://doi.org/10.3389/fvets.2021.621188.
6. Marcia P. Jimenez, et al., "Associations between Nature Exposure and Health: A Review of the Evidence," *International Journal of Environmental Research and Public Health* 18, no. 9: 4790, https://doi.org/10.3390/ijerph18094790.

7. Emily Anthes, *The Great Indoors: The Surprising Science of How Buildings Shape Our Behavior, Health, and Happiness* (Picador, 2020), 160.
8. D. King and C. Janiszewski, "Affect-gating," *Journal of Consumer Research* 38, no.4 (2011): 697–711, https://doi.org/10.1086/660811; M. Valentini, U. Kischka, and P. W. Halligan (2008). Residual haptic sensation following stroke using ipsilateral stimulation. *Journal of Neurology, Neurosurgery & Psychiatry* 79, no. 3, 266–70; A. K. Gulledge, M. Hill, Z. Lister, and C. Sallion (2007). Nonerotic physical affection: it's good for you. In low-cost approaches to promote physical and mental health (pp. 371–84). Springer, New York, NY; Gallace, A., & Spence, C. (2010). The science of interpersonal touch: an overview. *Neuroscience & Biobehavioural Reviews* 34, no. 2, 246–59.
9. David Barlas et al., "Comparison of the Auditory and Visual Privacy of Emergency Department Treatment Areas with Curtains Versus Those with Solid Walls," *Annals of Emergency Medicine* 38, no. 2 (2001): 135–39, https://doi.org/10.1067/mem.2001.115441.
10. Anjali Joseph, et al., "Realizing Improved Patient Care Through Human-centered Design in the OR (2021), Agency for Healthcare Research and Quality, https://ahrq.gov.
11. Veronika Kotradyova, et al. "Wood and Its Impact on Humans and Environment Quality in Health Care Facilities," 2019, International Journal of Environmental Research and Public Health 16, no. 18: 3496. https://doi.org/10.3390/ijerph16183496.

Chapter 16: Design for Better Community

1. See Rachel Hewitt, *In Her Nature: How Women Break Boundaries in the Great Outdoors* (Vintage, 2024); Martha Brady, "Creating Safe Spaces and Building Social Assets for Young Women in the Developing World: A New Role for Sports," *Women and Sports* 33, no. 1 and 2 (2005): 35–49, https://www.jstor.org/stable/40005500; "Plan Spaces to Encourage Equal Social Relations Between Men and Women," UN Women, last modified December 10, 2010, https://endvawnow.org/en/articles/381-plan-spaces-to-encourage-equal-social-relations-between-men-and-women.html.
2. David Hupin et al., "Even a Low-Dose of Moderate-to-Vigorous Physical Activity Reduces Mortality by 22% in Adults Aged ≥60 Years: A Systematic Review and Meta-Analysis," *British Journal of Sports Medicine* 49, no. 19 (2015): 1262–67, https://doi.org/10.1136/bjsports-2014-094306.
3. Researchers have found that the densest urban networks see a much higher share of walking and biking than less dense areas, which tends to translate to better health outcomes, such as lower rates of obesity, diabetes, and heart disease, than in more suburban layouts. See Wesley E. Marshall and Norman W. Garrick, "Effect of Street Network Design on Walking and Biking," *Transportation Research Record: Journal of the Transportation Research Board* 2198, no. 1 (2010): 103–15, https://doi.org/10.3141/2198-12.
4. In the U.S., between 50 to 60 percent of many cities' downtowns are dedicated to parking alone. Cars are large and take up a lot of space, which is why we have congestion and parking issues. When a person is standing, they occupy five square feet. When walking, roughly ten square feet. A car occupies 350 square feet when standing still (if you include access to the doors), and at thirty miles per hour with a couple car lengths' distance from other cars for safety, it occupies 1,000 square feet. So when you drive, you take up one hundred times more space than when you walk. See Brad Plumer, "Cars Take Up Way Too Much Space in Cities. New Technology Could Change That," Vox, accessed February 23, 2025, https://www.vox.com/a/new-economy-future/cars-cities-technologies.

5. Since the 1950s, Americans have viewed suburbs as the answer to a good life. But as time has passed, we've seen that suburbs are a blend of urban and rural without the advantages of either. You don't have easy access to shops, services, and civic institutions like in a city. Nor do you get acres and acres of land to farm on. Suburban homes take up land like ranches used to, but don't make use of the land agriculturally. It's a waste. Especially the way suburbs are laid out, you can't make use of the land around homes.

   It might be smarter to build houses closer and then pool the small bits of land together into actual arable land. To achieve gentle density, we can't have freestanding houses because they'd have to be so close that the open space left over is essentially narrow rings around each house, which is useless space. As James Howard Kunstler mentions in his TED Talk on the tragedy of the suburbs, we're coming to the end of the cheap oil era and will have to try something else: We'll need to downscale and resize, living closer to where we work and closer to each other. See Kunstler, "The Ghastly Tragedy of the Suburbs," *TED Talk*, Monterey, CA, February 2004, https://www.ted.com/talks/james_howard_kunstler_the_ghastly_tragedy_of_the_suburbs.
6. The ideas on rotating row houses so their long sides face the street and the housing hills that terrace back were both influenced by the patterns observed and explained by architect and theorist Christopher Alexander in *A Pattern Language* (Oxford University Press, 1977).
7. Most businesses in the U.S. today, including industrial operations, are compatible with residential uses, so it's entirely feasible for them to be mixed into neighborhoods, not segregated in commercial districts.

Chapter 17: The World That Awaits Us

1. Michael Mehaffy and Nikos A. Salingaros, "The Architect Has No Clothes," Guernica, October 19, 2011, https://www.guernicamag.com/the_architect_has_no_clothes/.

ABOUT THE AUTHOR

Danish Kurani believes that architecture changes the quality of our lives. He is devoted to teaching people about the power of design and to building environments for human wellness.

He has designed schools, homes, institutions, offices, parks, and community spaces across four continents, improving life for over 30,000 people. *Fast Company* named him one of the world's most innovative architects.